THE

INDUS DELTA COUNTRY

THE INDUS DELTA COUNTRY

A MEMOIR

CHIEFLY ON ITS ANCIENT GEOGRAPHY AND HISTORY

MAJOR-GENERAL M. R. HAIG, M.R.A.S

GYAN

Published by

GYAN

Gyan Publishing House
5, Ansari Road
Daryaganj, New Delhi-110002
Phone: 011-47034999, 9811692060
E-mail: books@gyanbooks.com

Distribution Network
gyanbooks.com
India, USA, Canada, UK, Australia, France

ISBN: 978-81-212-9134-7 (PB)
First Published, 1894

2nd Impression 2023

Printed at: Gyan Press, Delhi.

THE INDUS DELTA COUNTRY
AUTHOR: MAJOR-GENERAL M. R. HAIG

THE

INDUS DELTA COUNTRY

A MEMOIR

CHIEFLY ON ITS ANCIENT GEOGRAPHY AND HISTORY

BY

MAJOR-GENERAL M. R. HAIG, M.R.A.S.

WITH THREE MAPS

LONDON
KEGAN PAUL, TRENCH, TRÜBNER & CO., LTD.
PATERNOSTER HOUSE, CHARING CROSS ROAD
1894

THE
INDUS DELTA COUNTRY

PREFACE.

THE first two sections of the following Memoir were written and printed seven years ago. Since then a few copies have been privately circulated among friends who are interested in the subjects of which it treats. Within the last year the original plan of the little work has been carried to completion, but under the disadvantage of distance from large libraries and the consequent impossibility of refreshing my acquaintance with works—especially Oriental works—which it would have been desirable to consult anew. I have thus been obliged to depend in great measure on the resources of a very modest library, on notes and extracts made when opportunities were more favourable, and, in the last resort, on a memory for which I am obliged to ask the reader's most indulgent consideration.

The Memoir pretends to be nothing more than a rough guide for those in Sindh, who, taking an interest in the past of a province, one of the poorest, and in its outward aspect the least lovely in India, care to seek out the relics of former ages, and trace for themselves some picture of the country as it was at different periods of its generally troubled history.

The pressure under which the governmental machine works in India grows more and more intense; leisure becomes less; books, more than a few, are not for the nomad official: hence the convenience of a *compendium* of any kind — even of the rough and makeshift kind—for those who, if they pursue any branch of inquiry, must pursue it under difficulties unknown to the leisured student in other lands. That which is here offered as a humble aid to research has only such value as may be supposed to attach to the results of considerable local knowledge, to careful consideration of questions discussed, and to a sincere endeavour to arrive at truth in matters great or small. Its literary form requires much apology. For this and its many other defects I trust the indulgence of the reader will not be wanting.

M. R. H.

DAVOS PLATZ, SWITZERLAND,
November, 1894.

CONTENTS.

I. SKETCH OF THE GEOGRAPHY AND HYDROGRAPHY OF THE DELTA COUNTRY 1

II. THE DELTA AT THE TIME OF ALEXANDER'S EXPEDITION . . . 8

III. THE DELTA ACCORDING TO LATER GREEK ACCOUNTS 23

IV. THE DELTA ACCORDING TO THE ACCOUNTS OF EARLY EASTERN WRITERS 34

V. EASTERN GEOGRAPHERS ON CENTRAL AND LOWER SINDH . . . 65

VI. THE DELTA COUNTRY AFTER THE SECOND MUHAMMEDAN INVASION OF INDIA 72

VII. THE PORTUGUESE IN THE DELTA 97

VIII. THE CAMPAIGN OF THE IMPERIAL FORCES IN LOWER SINDH IN 1591-92 102

IX. LOWER SINDH IN THE MODERN PERIOD 110

APPENDICES 124

MAPS.

I. THE KARĀCHĪ COAST IN THE TIME OF ALEXANDER THE GREAT.

II. SKETCH MAP OF PATALENE.

III. INDUS DELTA COUNTRY.

CORRIGENDA.

Page 6, line 9, for 1500 read 1700.

„ 13. „ 27, for Morontobaros read Morontobara.

Map III., for Rishul (name of river mouth) read Richhal.

THE INDUS DELTA COUNTRY.

I.

SKETCH OF THE GEOGRAPHY AND HYDROGRAPHY OF THE DELTA COUNTRY.

A POPULAR geographical notion of its inhabitants distinguishes three main divisions of the Lower Indus Valley. These are named *Siro*, or "Upper Country;" *Vicholo*, or Middle Country; and *Lāṟu*, or "Sloping, descending (to the sea) Country," and correspond respectively to Upper Sindh, or the country north of about 27° N. lat., 40 miles above Sēwaṇ; Central Sindh, or the tract between that limit and Ḫaydarābād; and Lower Sindh, extending from Ḫaydarābād to the sea. This last division may be treated as the historical Delta country of the Indus, that is, the Delta country as seen when the light of history first falls upon it in the descriptions of the writers on Alexander's expedition. At that period the head of the Delta was at Patala, where the river divided into two large branches, running, one south-east, the other south-west, to the sea, and each retaining the name Indus. Any precise identification of the site of Patala is hardly within the limits of possibility. I am unable to agree with the authorities who would place it at Ḫaydarābād, or with others who think Ṭhaṭa a more likely situation; but there are grounds, as we shall see, for the conjecture that it lay not very far below the latitude of the former town, though considerably to the east of its longitude. It seems, therefore, legitimate to assume that the Sindhī geographical division of "Lāṟu" is nearly identical with Patalene, or the Delta country of the Indus as known to the Greeks.

The Delta tract of this memoir, then, extends from the sea northward to the latitude of Ḫaydarābād, or 25° 23′ N., and is bounded on the east by the sandhills of the desert, by the farthest eastern channel of the Indus, known as the Purāṇ, which has long ceased to carry water except in times of unusually high floods, and by the Korī Mouth or Creek, which separates the Delta from Kaꞔhꞔhha; on the west by the outer border of the plains, formed of hill débris, sloping eastward and southward from the Kohistān or mountainous region of Sindh. Here the boundary runs south by west for 50 miles to within a short distance from Ṭhaṭa, where it turns almost due west, and continues for 60 miles more to the sea near Karāchī. The Delta region thus defined contains an area of nearly 10,000 square miles, the length of its different sides being—on the north, from the Indus west of Ḫaydarābād to Umarkoṭ, 90 miles; on the east, from Umarkot to the mouth of the Khorī Creek, 150 miles; on the west, from Ḫaydarābād to near Ṭhaṭa, and thence to the south-eastern point of Clifton sands near Karāchī, 110 miles; and the coast-line, 125 miles.

This alluvial tract is everywhere furrowed by ancient river channels, some continuous throughout the Delta region, and for many miles above it, but very many others in a more or less obliterated condition, and traceable but for short distances. Among the former we find on the extreme eastern border a channel with a very old and interesting history. This is the *Hākṟo*, which skirts the sandhills and runs into the Purāṇ about 20 miles north of the Ran of Kachchha. Hākṟo is a name in modern times restricted to the lower part of what has become a flood-channel of the Indus, and is now known as the Nārā (officially, Eastern Nārā), but it once belonged to an entirely independent river, of which the Nārā channel formed a part.[1] The course of this river, may be traced throughout Sindh, in the far north of which it bears the name of *Wandan;* through Bahāwalpūr where the name *Hākra* or *Hakra* reappears, but is eventually replaced by that of *Sūdharah* and others; thence through the north of Bīkānīr, and onward beyond Rājputāna to the foot of the Himālaya. The opinion that this "lost river," as it has been called, was no other than the Satlaj, which some centuries ago forsook its original bed not far from the point where it leaves the mountains, and turning north-westward into the valley of the Biyāh, eventually mingled its waters with those of the latter river, has been ably maintained by a writer in the *Calcutta Review.*[2] Whether this has

[1] *Nārā* is merely a Sindhī modification, by the common process of substituting *r* for *l*, of *Nālā* (vulg. *Nullah*), a "torrent-bed," "flood-channel," &c.

[2] No. cxvii., vol. lix., 1874, "The Lost River of the Indian Desert."

been proved or not, it is certain that the Hākro of Lower Sindh was formerly a part of the course of an independent stream, the drying up of which has been calamitous, not only in reducing thousands of square miles of once fertile land and inhabited country to waste and solitude, but also in forcing a vast additional body of water into the already overcharged channel of the Indus, thus enormously increasing the risk of desolating floods along the lower course of that river.

Four or five miles west of the Hākro, and for a long distance parallel with it, lies an old channel of the Indus called the Badahrī, which enters the Purāṇ about 18 miles north of the confluence of the Hākro with the latter. This also is now a mere flood-channel, and is connected with the Hākro; but the upper portion of its course, much silted up, and after some miles disappearing altogether, comes from the north-west in such a direction as to indicate that, when flowing, it must have left the main river at some bifurcation in Central Sindh. As other portions of old channels trending in the same direction, and probably remnants of the branch to which the Badahrī belonged, are found not far south-east of the conjectured site of the Arab capital Manṣūra, it is not unlikely that this channel is the one described by El-Birūnī as leaving the Indus at Manṣūra and running east (south-east) to the border of Kachchha. Its name, he says, was *Sind Sāgar*.[3]

But the most important of all the forsaken channels of the Indus is the *Purāṇ*. This can still be clearly traced from two different starting-points in Central Sindh, one 24, the other 36 miles north-east of Haydarābād. The two head-channels run south-east for about 50 miles, and unite at a spot 45 miles east by south from Haydarābād, whence the single channel has a course first south and then south-west of over 140 miles to the head of the Korī Creek, the last 50 miles being through the Ran of Kachchha. The lower part of the channel in Sindh is still half a mile broad in some places, and for a long distance the average breadth is perhaps a quarter of a mile. West of the Purāṇ we find many ancient channels, some of which are of considerable length, while many are mere fragments of former courses of the river. Among the former is one which has now no general name, various portions of it being distinguished by appellations evidently of modern date, and known only within a limited area. Its head-waters, like those of the Purāṇ,

[3] Sir H. Elliot's "History of India," i. 49. The question of the site of Manṣūra has been discussed by the author in the *Journal of the Royal Asiatic Society*, vol. xvi., part 2.

seem to have run in two streams, the more northern of which left the Indus in the lower part of Central Sindh. This channel joins the Purāṇ about 10 miles north of the Ran of Kachchha. For convenience-sake it will be called in this memoir the "Western Purāṇ." Still farther west, at an average distance of about 12 miles, we come upon the *Rēn,* a branch which left the Indus at a point 25 miles south east of Ḫaydarābād, and had a course generally south of over 80 miles into the Ran, a little within the Sindh border. Whether its waters here spread over the Ran, or eventually made a channel for themselves into the sea, I am not aware, but the surveyors have not traced the channel beyond a depression in the Sindh Ran. The Rēn may be called modern, as it dried up so late as the middle of last century, when the Indus suddenly abandoned its course some miles above Naṣrpūr, and struck into its present line west of Haydarābād. It seems not to have been a very large branch; the local historians, indeed, apply the Persian term *Jū'ībār* to it, indicating a small stream. Parts of its channel are now occupied by the *Gūnī*, a continuation of the *Phulēlī*, which leaves the Indus 10 miles north of Ḫaydarābād: other parts have been utilised as irrigational canals. The Rēn, as we shall see, is of some historical interest in connection with the wanderings of the Emperor Humāyūn in Sindh during the darkest period of his fortunes. Farther west again, at a distance varying from 15 to 35 miles, is the *Gūngro.* The upper portion of this channel is not now distinctly traceable; I mean, its original head-channel, for the Gūngro is now an irrigational canal, and derives its supply from courses opened in comparatively recent times. It probably issued from the Indus some miles below the head of the Rēn branch. Its course is generally south, and it reaches the sea by the long tidal channel known as the *Sīr Mouth;* the total length of Gūngro and Sīr being about 120 miles. On its right bank the Gūngro is joined by the *Pīnyārī*, which leaves the Indus some miles south of the town of Jhirk (better known to Europeans under the corrupted name *Jerruck*); but this portion of the course of the Indus is, as will presently be explained, of modern date, and the Pīnyārī, as a branch of it, calls for no further notice. Near the latitude of Ṭhaṭa the Gūngro runs for some miles through the bed of what must have been a far older branch, the course of which is here nearly due east and west, but is not traceable for more than 8 or 10 miles. This small remnant of what, judging from its size, must once have been the main bed of the Indus, possesses some interest from the fact that the city of *Tūr*, the capital of the Sūmra chiefs when they held sway in Lower Sindh, was situated on its southern bank. There is reason to suppose, as will be seen hereafter, that this channel dried up in the early part of the fourteenth century.

West of the Gūngro, lying between it and the present course of the Indus, is the lower portion of that channel, which has been mentioned as having dried up on a sudden shifting of the Indus westward about the middle of last century. If a map of Sindh be examined, it will be noticed that at about 25 miles north by east of Ḥaydarābād the river, which has hitherto been flowing in a south-easterly direction, curves sharply to the west towards the village of Unarpūr, and then runs south and south-west. It was at this point that the change of course took place. For many years previously the river, continuing its south-easterly direction, had run by Naṣrpūr, which was on the left bank, and then south to the point where the Rēn left it, whence it turned south-west towards Ṭhaṭa. It is known that this channel finally dried up in 1758, but it is said that it began to fail a few years earlier, the river apparently taking a little time to force its whole volume into the new course. The entire length of the abandoned channel, now known as the *Phiṭo*,[4] is considerably over 100 miles, its greatest distance from the present course of the river being about 20 miles. For the last 60 miles its course is no longer continuous, but may be traced by its numerous remnants, while the northern half is clearly defined throughout nearly its entire extent.[5] Twelve miles north of the head of the Rēn another channel, called the *Mābān*, leaves the Phiṭo, and runs south-east. Its course has not been traced by the surveyors for more than about 25 miles, but it probably joined the Western Purāṇ. The head of the Mābān is situated in the midst

[4] The word means "*abandoned*," and is frequently applied to dried-up channels.

[5] It was on this channel, about 10 miles above Naṣrpūr, and near the village of *Bohirī* (in the local histories generally, but erroneously, written *Lohirī*), that Jānī Beg. Tarkhān, the ruler of Lower Sindh, intrenched his forces during the campaign of 1591–92, and for two months resisted all the assaults of Akbar's army, commanded by Mīrzā 'Abdu'r-Raḥīm, his Khān-i-Khānān. Such was the strength of the position, and so clever the tactics of the Sindhian chief, who, possessing a numerous fleet and complete command of the river, was able to supply his own troops with ease, while, by raising the peasantry against the invaders, he succeeded in cutting off their convoys and menacing them with starvation, that the imperialist commander had at length to abandon the investment, and retire till his opponent could be lured out of the intrenchments.

of a vast area of blown sand, a circumstance which always indicates the former existence of a large bifurcation. Another tract of blown sand, but a much smaller one, is found at the head of the Rēn.

Passing still westward, we come to the present channel of the Indus. This divides the Lower Delta region [6] into two unequal portions. Of these, the western and much the smaller portion is in the form of an equilateral triangle, having sides of about 64 miles in length, consisting of the river, the coast-line, and the southern edge of the Kohistān plains, and including an area of about 1500 square miles. This it will be convenient to call the "Western Delta," a name the more suitable that all the westward flowing branches of the river have, or have once had, their mouths within the limits of the tract to which it will apply. Here there are only two branches which call for notice—the *Baghāṟ* and the *Ghāṟo*. The former has its head in the Indus 6 miles south of Ṭhaṭa, whence it runs through the middle of the Western Delta, and communicates with the sea by several mouths, as the *Rishul, Shīshā, Pītī-ānī, Kkūdī*, and *Pītī*. The name Baghāṟ properly belongs to the channel only as far as the head of the Shīshā mouth. Beyond this point the westward prolongation of the channel is known by various names in different portions of its course, such as *Khārā* (Brackish), *Rāho*, and others. The Pītī mouth, the farthest western embouchure of the Baghāṟ, is 12 miles south-east of Karāchī. The Baghāṟ is now merely a flood-channel, but it appears to have been for several centuries the chief western branch of the Indus, and it was a perennial stream so late as the early years of this century. The *Ghāṟo* runs nearly east and west along the southern border of the Kohistān, and is thus on the extreme edge of the Delta. Its course, which is about 40 miles in length, is, in fact, the last portion of what was once a large branch of the Indus. Another portion of this branch is found farther east in the *Kalrī*, now a flood-channel of the Indus, which it leaves a few miles north-east of Ṭhaṭa, and, flowing westward for some distance, eventually turns south, and joins the Baghāṟ. The gap between the Kalrī and Ghāṟo is not more than 10 or 12 miles, and remnants of the old channel are found within it. The present southern course of the Kalrī appears to have been formed by the original stream having burst from its left (southern) bank at a point about 7 miles west of Ṭhaṭa, and forced a way for itself into

[6] That is, the tract south of about 24° 49′ N. lat., where the Indus leaves the Kohistān.

the Baghar. West of this point the old channel then silted up for a few miles, and the lowest portion, kept open by the action of the tide, became a mere creek.

To complete this portion of our subject, there remains to consider the interesting question of the secular extension of the Delta seaward. The various surveys of the coast which have been made during the last half century, and especially those carried out since the British conquest of Sindh (1843), have shown that at the main embouchure of the river for the time being the advance of the banks seaward goes on at a surprisingly rapid rate. Thus, when the last survey took place (in the early part of 1877) it was found that during the ten years which had elapsed since the preceding survey the banks at the river mouth had advanced no less than 3⅛ G. miles, or at the rate of a third of a mile yearly. On the other hand, a marked diminution was discovered to have taken place in banks which, at the time of the previous survey, had lain immediately before a mouth of the river now no longer in action, the embouchure having moved farther westward; while at points beyond the immediate vicinity of the main river mouth the alteration of soundings was found to be very slight.[7] There is thus an immense gain of land on the sea at one particular point; but this point is ever shifting, and on the occurrence of each change the sea wins back a large proportion of its lost territory. What the rate of permanent gain to the land may be in this incessant conflict of opposing forces it is difficult to estimate. The advance of the Nile Delta has been estimated to be at the rate of 4 metres or 4⅜ yards annually;[8] and the solid matter discharged by the river has been put at 240 millions of cubic yards per annum,[9] while that of the Indus has been estimated to be 217½ millions of cubic yards.[10] According to the relative depositing capabilities of the two rivers, as deduced from these estimates, the mean annual growth of the Indus Delta might be taken to be nearly four yards; but it is evident that the result thus obtained needs large modification when the counteracting effects of the sea, so much more powerful in the Indian Ocean than in the tideless Mediterranean,

[7] Report on the Survey of the Mouth of the Indus in March 1877, by Lieutenant Stiffe, late Indian Navy.

[8] Credner, Die Deltas. Petermann's Mittheilungen, Ergänzungsheft, No. 56, s. 25.

[9] *Edinburgh Review*, January 1877, "Mediterranean Deltas."

[10] By Colonel Tremenheere, R.E., when chief engineer in Sindh. *Journal R. G. S.*, xxxvii. p. 70.

are allowed for, and no doubt the advance of the Delta of the Indus has been very much slower than that of the Nile Delta. It must be remembered, however, that the rate of progress of nearly all Deltas is not constant, but varies greatly at different periods;[11] and if the annual growth of the Nile Delta in the present age is estimated at something more than four yards, there appears to be ground for believing that in earlier ages it was at times greatly in excess of that amount. The writer in the *Edinburgh Review*, above referred to, adduces historical evidence to show that up to a certain point in its progress the Nile Delta advanced at the rate of 29 yards per annum. In the space of 2300 years its growth was 33 G. miles, or 38 statute miles. It is probable that the Indus Delta has grown under similar conditions, though always at a much slower rate. Unfortunately historical evidence in this case is of so precarious a character as to afford ground for little beyond conjectures more or less plausible. Such as it is, however, it may be worth while to examine it. It will accordingly come under review in the following section.

II.

THE DELTA AT THE TIME OF ALEXANDER'S EXPEDITION (325–326 B.C.)

ARRIAN'S narrative of the voyage of Nearchus furnishes the fullest information we have of the geography of the Lower Delta at that time, though unfortunately it leaves very much to be desired. It will be well, in the first place, to remind the reader of his description of the first few days' navigation. I translate from C. Müller's edition of the "Indike," in his "Geographi Græci Minores," vol. i.:—"Weighing from the naval station, they came to anchor the first day in a large channel[12] of the Indus, where they stayed two days. The place was named Stoura, and was about a hundred stadia from the naval station. On the third day they weighed, and sailed 30 stadia to another channel, where the water was now salt, for the sea

[11] See Credner, *ut sup.*, I. Theil. 7, "Maas des Wachsthums der Deltas."

[12] The διώρυχες which the Greeks met with in the Lower Delta were certainly not *canals*, as some have supposed, but natural channels which intersect the land near the coast in all directions. A canal, and one large enough to hold a fleet, would have been a phenomenon indeed.

ran up it, especially during the flood-tide, and the (salt) water remained mingled with that of the river, even at the ebb. The place was named Kaumana. Continuing from this their course down river for 20 stadia, they came to anchor at Koreatis, still in the river. Starting hence, they sailed but a short space, for a bar appeared at the spot where the Indus discharged itself into the sea; the waves too were breaking violently on the coast, and the coast itself was rugged. However, in a part of the bar which was soft they made a cutting for a space of 5 stadia, and through this, when the tide flowed again, they conducted the vessels. Then sailing a winding course (along the coast) for 150 stadia, they came to anchor at Krokala, a sandy island, where they remained the following day. Near this dwell the Indian tribe called Arabies, whom I have mentioned in my larger work, stating also that they have their name from the river Arabis which runs through their country and falls into the sea, separating their territory from that of the Oritæ. From Krokala they sailed, having on their right the hill called by them Eiros, and on the left a low flat island. This island, stretching along the face of the coast, rendered the (intervening) creek narrow. Clearing through this, they came to anchor in a commodious harbour, and as it struck Nearchus as spacious and fine, he named it 'Alexander's Haven.' At the harbour mouth, at a distance of about 2 stadia, there is an island named Bibakta, but the whole region is called Sangada. This island, placed as a barrier against the sea, caused the existence of the harbour."

There is reason to believe that the western branch of the Indus explored by Alexander, and from which Nearchus started on his voyage, was that of which the present Ghāṟo Creek formed the lowest portion. It is curious that though so much pains were bestowed on the exploration of the two main arms of this river, no mention should have been made of any minor branch. Yet it is impossible for any one acquainted with the hydrography of the Delta to doubt that there must have been many such in existence then, as at all times, or that, it being the period of high flood, some of them were navigable and of a size to render them deserving of notice. It seems most probable, however, from the large estimates of the distance between the mouths of the main arms of that day formed by some of those who took part in the expedition, that these arms were the extreme eastern and extreme western channels of the Delta. The estimates were 115, 206, and 230 miles,[13] the *lowest* being almost exactly the direct distance between the mouths of these channels (the Korī and the Ghāṟo), as ascertained by recent survey. Further, some of the circumstances described in the passage above translated supply irresistible evidence, as I think, that it was through the Ghāṟo that Nearchus sailed into the sea. In that passage it is stated that there was a bar (ἕρμα) at the mouth of the river. This may mean either a reef or a bar of sand and mud, such as is found at all the river mouths, though the former is, I believe, the more usual meaning of the word. If we are to understand that the obstruction at the mouth of the river was caused in part by rock, it is certain that that mouth cannot have been situated to the east of the Ghāṟo, for along the whole sea-border of the Delta, to a depth of several miles, no rock, not even a stone, is to be found. This fact so impressed Sir A. Burnes, when in the Delta in 1831, that, on observing what he took to be a rock in the Pītī channel (immediately east of the Ghāṟo), he without hesitation identified it with the obstacle that had stopped Nearchus. He says: "Near the mouth of the river we passed a rock stretching across the stream, which is particularly mentioned by Nearchus, who calls it a 'dangerous rock,' and is the more remarkable, since there is not even a stone below Tatta in any other part of the Indus." [14] Had he really seen a rock, there would have been much to say in favour of his identification; but when, a few years after the British conquest of Sindh, a survey of the Indus mouths was carried out, special inquiries were made for Sir Alexander's rock, with the result of ascertaining that nothing of the kind existed. He had evidently mistaken an oyster-bank, such as is found occasionally in the tidal creeks, for rock, which these banks resemble.[15] The narrative further tells us that the coast outside the river mouth was *rugged* or *rocky* (τραχέα). Now, such an epithet would be utterly out of place if applied to the low mudbanks of the actual Delta coast, but would be quite appropriate as a description of that southern border of the Kohistān plain consisting of a compact gravelly soil, frequently broken by outcropping rock, and furrowed

[13] Estimate of Aristobulus, 1000 stadia; of Nearchus, 1800 stadia; of Onesicritus, 2000 stadia.

[14] Travels into Bokhara, iii. 16. Rock crops up in the Delta some miles below Ṭhaṭa, but none exists, I think, within 35 miles of the coast.

[15] Mr. Fenner's Report on his survey of the tidal channels (in the Western Delta) of the Indus in 1848.

by the courses of hill-torrents, which, well elevated above sea-level, bounds the Delta between Karāchī and Thata, and forms, it may be said, the northern bank of the Ghāṛo. At the present day the Delta extends along this ridge westward as far as Gisrī, near Karāchī; but it is probable, as will appear, that at the time of Nearchus's voyage the ridge for some miles east of Gisrī Creek was washed by the sea. Again, we are told that after leaving the river the fleet ran a *winding course* (εκπεριπλώσαντες), or, as Mr. M'Crindle well interprets it, "followed the winding of the coast."[16] But had the fleet issued from any of the mouths east of the Ghāro, there would have been no windings to follow. The only coast then would have been that of the Delta, which is singularly straight and regular, the result of wave-action on its plastic material, and the course accordingly must have been shaped straight. On the other hand, leaving the Indus by the Ghāṛo mouth and keeping inshore, as it almost always did during the voyage, the fleet would be compelled to run a winding course in conformity with the irregular contour of the coast which it was following. The little descriptive details here mentioned forcibly suggest that the narrative reproduces on these occasions the actual words of the eye-witness from whom they were derived, and that in these passages Arrian copies verbatim Nearchus's account of incidents which must have been indelibly impressed on his memory. In the rugged shore lashed by the waves of the Indian Ocean, in the winding course run, we have no doubt a faithful picture, and it can hardly represent any other part of the Sindh coast than that which I have here described.

But before leaving for the moment the subject of the Delta, there is one point which deserves notice. It seems unaccountable that at the mouth of one of the principal arms of the Indus, and at a time of the year, probably September, when the periodical flood could not have wholly subsided, there should not be water enough on the bar, even at high tide (which at this part of the coast rises 7 feet at neaps and 9 feet at springs), to allow of the fleet's passing out till the channel had been artificially deepened. I am inclined to think that the explanation of this difficulty may be that on approaching the sea Nearchus led his fleet out of the main stream (possibly to avoid the current which at ebb-tide runs with tremendous violence at the larger Indus mouths) and through some one of the

[16] The Commerce and Navigation of the Erythræan Sea, p. 176.

side channels which the larger streams throw off in the vicinity of the sea. Such a side channel of the Ghāṛo actually exists, and is known as the Kudro. It runs, moreover, close under the rocky ridge which has been described, and its mouth may therefore have been obstructed, as we can readily understand, by some reef projecting into its bed. Near the present mouth of this creek there is a small port named Wāghūḍar (Crocodile-hole), used by river-boats of light draught.

The question of the particular channel by which the fleet reached the sea being thus disposed of, the point next to be determined is the position of Krokala, as we have a measurement from the mouth of the river to that island which will help us to fix the line of the Delta coast at the time referred to. It will serve, however, to clear the way if we identify Alexander's Haven out of its order in the narrative. That Karāchī harbour, or rather Karāchī Bay, of which the modern harbour is an artificially limited portion, is Alexander's Haven, is generally admitted. Here, in fact, there is no choice of positions, for there is no other protected anchorage for seagoing vessels in all this region, far less any harbour which could be described as "kalos" and "euormos." Now it is quite clear from the narrative that Krokala was close to Alexander's Haven. Contrary to the regular habit of the narrator, no distance is given from Krokala, and we may infer that it was too short to be worth mentioning. Further, the fleet seems to have entered a creek immediately on quitting Krokala, and through this to have run into Alexander's Haven. It is thus evident that the two points were at no distance apart. But on leaving the island the fleet had a hill called Eiros on the right. The word "oros" is applied by Arrian to the cliff, or hill, or high ground, or whatever it was, that was named Eiros, and the word has always been rendered by his translators *mountain*; but as nothing that by any stretch of imagination can be called a mountain exists within 25 miles of even the present coast of the Delta, it is evident that whatever Eiros was, it was not a mountain. We must, therefore, assume the modified meaning of "hill," or "headland," or "high ground." Any of these would be applicable to Manora, which is the most prominent feature on this part of the coast, though its highest point is but 100 feet above the sea. General Cunningham accordingly finds Eiros in Manora, and says that to have Eiros on the right and a low flat island on the left would be a very accurate description of the entrance to Karāchī harbour; but he forgot that it would only be accurate as a description of the bearings in the case of a vessel *leaving* the harbour, for a vessel entering has Manora on the *port* side. This disposes of Manora. There remain only two other hills or headlands in all this tract of coast. One of these, called "Clifton" by the English and "Hawa-Bandar" by the natives, is the eastern headland of Karāchī Bay; the other is Gisrī, a mile east of Clifton. Clifton I believe to be Eiros. The "narrow creek" would then be Chinī Creek,[17] which runs under Clifton ridge into Karāchī Bay and harbour, and the "low island" Kīāmārī Flat, which *stretches along the mainland opposite Clifton ridge, and renders the intervening creek narrow.* Manora exactly answers to Bibakta in this respect, that, *being placed as a barrier against the sea, it gives rise to Karāchī harbour;* but I must admit my inability to make that other part of the description, "at the harbour mouth at a distance of 2 stadia," fit in with this identification. Manora is three-quarters of a mile or 6 stadia distant from Kīāmārī, at the nearest point. Moreover, it is not now an island, but is connected with the mainland to the west by a narrow ridge of sand some 10 miles in length. It should be mentioned that there are indications of some elevation of the land having occurred along this part of the coast. Mr. Blanford, when conducting the Geological Survey of the neighbourhood, found evidence near Cape Monze (Rās Mu'ārī) of "elevation of the land having taken place at no distant period."[18] Indications of a rise of the land were also observed by him along the coast to the west of Cape Monze,[19] and this may explain the total disappearance of the harbour called by Arrian Morontobaros, which appears to have been but a few miles east of the modern Sōn Mi'āṇī, and is described as "large, well shut-in, deep, and still." Evidence to the same effect is found in the vicinity of Karāchī, where the sea now never reaches the high-water mark of former times. To this fact was no doubt owing the abandonment of a port the site of which was at the island, or rather mound, rising out of the surrounding mud, on which Karāchī Observatory stands. Here, according to native accounts, stood a substantially-built town, with a harbour, reached by a branch

[17] The mouth of Chinī Creek was closed some years ago in connection with the works carried out for the improvement of Karāchī harbour.

[18] Memoirs of the Geological Survey of India, vol. xvii. p. 184.

[19] Ibid., p. 191.

of the Chinī Creek, and resorted to by ships from various neighbouring countries. It is said to have been flourishing 400 years ago.[20] The sea has now receded so much from the site that it could not be reached by a rowboat.

But it is time to close this digression and return to Krokala. This, I believe, no longer exists, at least as an island. Whether through the elevation of the land or the silting up of the intervening channel, Krokala has, according to my theory, become part of the mainland, and is to be found in that sandy spit of land, or a portion of it, which projects south-eastward, in line with the present Delta coast, for some three miles from the bluffs of Clifton and Gisrī. Consistently with the evidence, it seems to me hardly possible to find Krokala in any other position than this. The narrative plainly conveys that the fleet, *on starting from the island*, had Eiros on the right.[21] Krokala and Eiros were, therefore, only a short distance apart, and I infer that there was but a narrow seaway north of the island to be traversed by the fleet before it ran under the headland of Clifton into Chinī Creek. Dr. Vincent and General Cunningham have identified Krokala with Kīāmārī,[22] which indeed is a "sandy island," but will be found by anybody who follows the narrative closely, and with the aid of a correct map of the coast about Karāchī, to have no other claim whatever to be regarded as the Krokala of Nearchus. On the other hand, it does correspond very exactly to the description of that other island which the fleet had on its left when passing through the "narrow creek" below Eiros into Alexander's Haven. The suggestion that, in the lapse of so many centuries, Krokala has become part of the mainland, seems to me to involve no improbability—nothing more out of the common than the shoaling and sanding-up of a perhaps narrow channel. Clifton sands have no doubt been formed to a great extent by deposit brought down by the Malīr river, a hill-torrent which drains a very wide area of the Kohistān, and, when in flood, pours a tremendous mass of water heavily laden with silt into the sea through the Gisrī Creek. If I am right in my view as to the position of Krokala, that island must have been a creation of the Malīr; for, being 150 stadia from the mouth of the Indus, it could not have owed its existence to the latter river. Whatever sea-space

[20] MSS. notes by a native merchant of Karāchī.

[21] Ἐκ δὲ Κρωκάλων ἐν δεξιῇ μὲν ἔχοντες τὸ καλεόμενον αὐτοῖσιν Εἶρουν . . . ἔπλωον.

[22] See Vincent's "Commerce and Navigation of the Ancients," i. 194 *et seq.*; and Cunningham's "Ancient Geography of India," pp. 306, 307.

there was between the island and the mainland may have been filled up gradually by Malīr silt and sea-sand, and the elevation of the coast would of course contribute to the same end.[23]

The position of Krokala being thus determined, in the only way, as it seems to me, to accord with the evidence, the coast-line of the Delta, as it was in those days, must be fixed by the measurement given between the two points, namely, 150 stadia. But here we meet with another difficulty in the extremely erroneous estimates of his runs which Nearchus made throughout the voyage. From Alexander's Haven to the frontier of Carmania these estimates are greatly in excess of the truth, and beyond that point they are far below it, as has been proved by the checks supplied by modern charts. So great is the excess of error during the first part of the voyage, that writers like D'Anville and Vincent have come to the conclusion that the estimates were based on some standard which they have taken to be about half the dimension of the Olympic stadium. It is obvious, however, that this hypothesis would meet the case of only one set of distances, and that consistency would require the assumption of an enlarged stadium to explain the error of defect in the other set. But, as pointed out by Mr. Bunbury, in his "History of Ancient Geography," there is no evidence whatever that any other than the ordinary stadium was in use among the Greeks, or known to them; and were it otherwise, the employment by a writer of different standards in different parts of the same work would be highly improbable.[24] The same high authority shows that there is some ground for suspecting Nearchus to have based one of the most important of all these estimates on the rough method of calculating a full day's run at 500 stadia, or 50 G. miles.[25] Such was, indeed, the common method in ancient times, though the standard distance of a day's voyage varied, and it may safely be assumed that Nearchus knew no other way of calculating his runs. We may take it, then,

[23] The name Krokala is, as might be expected, wholly unknown in the locality. The suggestion that it was a Greek corruption of Kakrāla (the name of an ancient division of the Delta), started by Pottinger and repeated by Burnes, is not without plausibility; but Kakrāla was a tract near the middle of the Delta, in the present Pargana of Ghorābārī, and fully 50 miles to the south-east of Karāchī. There is, I believe, no foundation for the statement that the country around Karāchī was ever called Kakrāla. At the time of Nearchus's voyage it bore the name of Sangada, as we are expressly informed.

[24] History of Ancient Geography, i. 544–545.

[25] Ibid., 531, note 8. See also p. 393.

that 150 stadia represent a run of somewhere about 3½ hours; and remembering that the fleet was contending against a rough sea and an adverse wind,[26] and that this was the first day's experience of the ocean, it can hardly be supposed that vessels impelled by oars would make a better rate of progress than 2½ miles an hour. The entire run, then, would be 9 miles, and this distance measured eastward from Clifton Spit round the "windings of the coast" will bring us to a point close to the hamlet of Wāghūḍar, which point is 8 miles in direct line from the coast of the Delta as laid down in 1869. Thus it may be conjectured that in the space of 2195 years (326 B.C. to 1869 A.D.) the advance of the Delta seaward has been 8 miles, or at the rate of rather more than 6 yards in a year. This is less than a fourth of the growth of the Nile Delta in a not much greater period of time.

From this conjectural determination of the coast-line of these days we may proceed to fix, alike conjecturally, the position of the "naval station" which was the point of departure of the expedition. This was a little more than 150 stadia from the mouth of the river, or almost exactly the same distance as from the mouth to Krokala. Here, however, the different nature of the navigation, that is to say, comparatively smooth water and a current powerfully aiding the efforts of the rowers, will call for a much smaller reduction of the estimated progress than in the case of the navigation in the open sea. It is possible, indeed, that the rate of progress in the river may have

[26] The south-west monsoon was still blowing, as is proved by the fact that the fleet was detained in Alexander's Haven for twenty-four days by continuous gales from the sea. Unless meteorological conditions have totally changed in these regions, here is proof positive that the date of Nearchus's departure from the Indus was earlier than most commentators suppose. This is variously computed as 2d October 326 B.C. and 21st September 325 B.C., and we have then to account for the occurrence of twenty-four days of "*high and continuous gales*," beginning either in the last days of September or at the end of the first week of October; that is to say, lasting during the period which is *invariably* the calmest in the whole year, as all who know Sindh can testify. The violence of the south-west monsoon is past by the middle of August, and a month later the wind drops almost entirely, though what is called the "Elephanta" storm occurs in September, lasting, however, but a few hours. I have no hesitation in saying that the occurrence of twenty-four days of continuous gales at the time of the year during which Nearchus is generally supposed to have been in Karāchī harbour is opposed to all modern experience of the meteorology of the Indian Ocean and its coasts. Dr. Vincent took these gales to have been the north-east monsoon, but that does not set in till November, and is never, I believe, experienced on the Sindh coast in so violent a form as continued gales for more than three weeks.

been *under*-estimated in consequence of these circumstances, though it may be well still to assume some exaggeration. I would then reduce the 17¼ miles—the true equivalent of 150 stadia—plus the small excess which has not been specified, to 15 miles, and thus fix the naval station at a point about a mile west of the mouth of the "Ghaghar" hill-torrent. Under the circumstances, suppressed by Arrian but revealed by Strabo, of the energetic hostility of the natives, which led to the hurried departure of Nearchus from Sindh, it is probable that the naval station, whither the Greeks must have withdrawn on finding their position at Patala no longer tenable, was not on the right bank of the river, that is, on the Kohistān plain, where it would have been exposed to attack, but in some one of the islands of the Lower Delta, formed by branch channels, where it would be comparatively secure. The other anchorages, which were but very short distances apart, must have been a few miles to the east of Wāghūḍar. It is needless to say that no names at all resembling Stoura, Kaumana, or Koreatis—themselves most probably gross corruptions—are now to be found in the locality.

From the vicinity of Krokala we have a measurement which will be of some service in fixing the position of Patala; for we learn from Arrian that near Krokala lay the eastern limit of the territory of the Arabies, and from Quintus Curtius that Alexander's army took nine days to march from Patala to this point. It is probable that the Malīr river—the most important natural feature in this region—would form a boundary between tribe and tribe, just as the Pūrāli (Arabis) bounded the Arabies on the west, and separated them from the Oritæ. The Malīr runs into the sea through the Gisrī Creek, and therefore close to the position which has been assigned to Krokala; so that it would be quite consistent with Arrian's statements and with all the probabilities of the case to take this stream as the tribal boundary, and some spot near its mouth as the point reached by Alexander in his ninth march from Patala. Now, Quintus Curtius says that from this point to the Arabis (Pūrālī) there were five marches,[27] and the actual distance is about 57 miles; so that here his day's march averaged about 11½ miles. But as the ground traversed is not throughout so level and easy for the soldier as the plains of Sindh, we may reasonably suppose a somewhat higher rate for the earlier marches, say 13 miles. This

[27] Quint. Curt., Lib. x., § 39.

will give us a measurement of 117 miles from the point named to Patala, and we have next to consider in what direction the measurement should be made. It may be assumed that Alexander would select that route for his large army which afforded the best supply of water; that he would, if possible, keep within easy reach of the river or one of its branches; and that, unless under some strong compulsion of circumstances, he would not march an unwieldy host across the comparatively waterless plain of the Kohistān. Patala was on the Indus, and close to a large bifurcation whence a large branch ran westward—the direction which the army was now to take. It seems obvious that the earlier part of the route would follow this branch. Now if, as we have some good ground to conjecture, the Kalrī and Ghāṟo formed the lower portion of this branch, it follows that the upper and now obliterated portion, lying between Patala and the present head of the Kalrī north-east of Ṭhaṭa, must have come from some point far out in the middle portion of the Upper Delta country. In other words, the bend of the river westward from Patala must have been gradual, as bends always are in streams which work their way through yielding alluvial soil. To suppose, with General Cunningham,[28] that Patala was at or near Ḥaydarābād, and yet that the western arm of the Indus is to be identified with the Ghāṟo, involves the position that the stream turned almost at right angles into the present Kalrī. But nothing short of meeting with rock, which does not exist here, could possibly cause such an abrupt deflection from the general direction of the river. A study of the hydrography of the Delta shows that as the Indus north of Ṭhaṭa has forced its bed westward, so below that town there has been from time to time a movement of the channel in the opposite direction. The stream, that is to say, has a tendency to straighten its course, and the constant pressure westward is compensated in the Lower Delta by sudden shiftings, at longer or shorter intervals, into channels farther east. Thus the identification of the Ghāṟo and Kalrī with the western branch of Alexander's time carries with it as a necessary consequence the conclusion that Patala was situated considerably east of the longitude of Ḥaydarābād; and if we measure 117 miles from the eastern border of the Arabies, that is, as I suggest, from the Malīr near Karāchī, along the Ghāṟo and Kalrī, and the *probable* upper

[28] Ancient Geography of India, p. 279 ff.

portion of the western branch, we shall find that the ancient capital of the Delta was most likely not far from a spot 35 miles south-east of Ḫaydarābād. Those who have identified Patala with Ḫaydarābād have overlooked the fact that the Indus reached the vicinity of that place so recently as the second half of last century, and that even a thousand years after Alexander's expedition, when the Arabs appeared on the scene, the river was still far to the east of the position they assign to the chief town of the Delta. Nothing, indeed, can be more misleading in connection with such a river as the Indus than to base arguments for particular identifications on the hydrographical circumstances of the present day; for it may be regarded as almost absolutely certain that hardly any channel now carrying water was in existence in the distant times referred to; and instead of seeking for very ancient sites along the present course of the river, we should rather assume that, wherever they may be, here, at all events, they are not to be found. As regards the Ṭhaṭa identification, it can easily be shown to satisfy no one of the conditions of the problem. One consideration alone is fatal to it. The effect of the tide must have been distinctly perceptible higher up the Delta than Ṭhaṭa twenty-two centuries ago, since it is perceptible as high up as that place now, or was so not many years ago, the rapid extension of the land at the mouth of the river, and consequent lengthening of the channel, having perhaps rendered the tidal rise less noticeable at this spot within the last few years. But it is quite clear that the effect of the tide was not apparent at Patala or anywhere in its vicinity, for it was not until Alexander and his exploring party had left that place far behind them that they became aware that such a phenomenon as the tidal flow existed. On this ground alone then it is certain that Patala cannot have been anywhere near Ṭhaṭa.

The spot upon which I have fixed as the probable position of Patala happens to be equidistant from both extremities of the Delta coast as supposed to have existed in Alexander's time, the direct measurement from point to point being about 106 miles in each case. This is also very nearly the length of the Delta base, and thus if we might combine the statement of Onesikritus that the Delta formed an equilateral triangle with the statement of Aristobulus that the base measured 1000 stadia (115 st. miles), we might be pretty certain of having determined the site of the capital with considerable accuracy. Unfortunately neither is Onesikritus regarded as a trustworthy authority, nor had he, or any one else in the expedition, the means or opportunity of forming anything but the roughest possible guess as to the shape and extent of the Delta. All, therefore, that we may legitimately infer from their statements is that there was no considerable difference between the lengths of the two branch streams, and that the mouths of these were very far apart, each almost certainly at an extremity of the Delta base.

Various suggestions have been made in regard to the true name of the town which the Greeks called Patala. It seems to me, however, that the question has been solved by the tradition discovered in Tibet by the gifted and laborious Csoma de Körös, who has thus recorded it: "Potala or Potalaka (Tib. Gru-hdsin, or vulgo Kru-dsin, Boat-receiver, a haven or port) is the name of an ancient city at the mouth of the Indus river, the residence of Ixwāku and his descendants of the Suryavamsa. Four young princes (who afterwards were surnamed Shākya), being banished from that city by their father, took refuge in Kosala on the banks of the Bhāgirathī river (in the modern province of Rohilkhand), and built the city of Capilavastu. The residence of the Dalai Lāma at Lassa (built about the middle of the twelfth century) is likewise called Potala, because Chenrezik, the patron of the Tibetans, the spiritual son of Amitābha, is said to have resided at Potala in ancient India, and to have visited Tibet from that place." [29] Whatever amount of credit may be allowed to this tradition, it cannot be doubted that it has at all events preserved for us the correct name of the ancient capital of the Delta—a name too simple in form for even Greeks to corrupt materially. Further, it seems to show that Potala was a foundation of very distant times indeed, and we may perhaps infer that it was one of the earliest Aryan settlements in the neighbourhood of the ocean.[30]

The eastern arm of the Indus, explored by Alexander immediately after returning to Patala from his first voyage to the Indian Ocean,

[29] *Journal Bengal Asiatic Society*, vol. vi. p. 349, where the above extract is quoted from Csoma de Körös' MSS. See also Csoma de Körös' own article in the same Society's Journal for August 1833, vol. ii. p. 385.

[30] In Map II. Patala is represented as situated between the two arms of the Indus, in conformity with the statement of Ptolemy that the place was in one of the islands formed by the river (Geog. Lib. vii. C. I., § 59). The courses of the Indus and its branches, as shown in this map, except the portion west of Ṭhaṭa, and the few miles of the Purān immediately north of the Ran of Kachchha, are, I need hardly say, purely conjectural.

was probably some channel running into the Purān, not many miles, perhaps, above the point where it enters the Ran, as represented in Map ii., the Purān being, as previously stated, the extreme eastern channel of the Indus, and, as its name indicates, of great antiquity. That the Ran itself was the *large lake* into which the eastern arm flowed admits of no doubt, and it is a highly interesting question whether it had at this time ceased to be a permanent inland sea or not. The voyagers themselves supposed it to be a lake formed by the discharge of the eastern branch of the Indus, and perhaps of other streams running into it; but they saw it during the very height of the south-west monsoon, at which season the Ran is under water even at the present day when the Indus has long ceased to send any portion of its waters into it, unless at times of exceptionally high flood. The Ran is in reality flooded during the period of the south-west monsoon only, and then by the sea being forced into it through the Gulf of Kachchha and the Korī Creek—mainly through the latter. But the water is everywhere shallow, and certainly *fish larger than those of the Mediterranean* could not now be found in it. It is possible, however, that the large fish seen by the Greeks may have been in the deeper Korī Creek, the upper part of which may have been regarded as a portion of the lake.

According to Lassen, the drying-up of the inland sea which once covered the Ran is referred to in the Mahā Bhārata, and described as a miraculous occurrence, and an act of vengeance for a misdeed of the god Varuna.[31] If Lassen is right in asserting that the myth refers to the Ran, and if the myth itself belongs to the Mahā Bhārata in its original form, and is not an addition of later times—points on which I am incompetent to form any opinion—there can be do doubt that the origin of the Ran is far older than the time of Alexander.[32] The local traditions, however, seem to show that the inland sea had existed to a much later period, and various places on the shores of the Ran are still spoken of by the natives as having formerly been *ports.*[33]

[31] "Indische Alterthumskunde," I. 546, n. 1., Edn. 1847, where the myth is given.

[32] The learned assign the date of the composition of the Mahā Bhārata to a period considerably later than that of Alexander (Weber's "History of Indian Literature," p. 186, and note 201*a* p. 187), but of course the myths and legends embodied in it are of much greater antiquity than the epic itself.

[33] See Sir A. Burnes' account of the Ran in the third volume of his travels into Bukhārā, and an article on the same subject by the late Sir Bartle Frere in the *Journal of the Royal Geographical Society*, vol. xl. pp. 194 ,195.

In the first century of our era the water in the Ran was shallow, according to the author of the "Periplus," who seems to have been accurately informed, since he correctly describes the Ran as divided into "Greater" and "Less."[34] The eastern or smaller Ran would appear to have been under water, and subject to the regular influx of the tide, in 1026, when Maḥmūd of Ghaznī, after capturing Somnāth, pursued a Hindu chief who had taken refuge in one of the islands of North-Eastern Kachchh. Maḥmūd was warned that in attempting to reach this island he might be overwhelmed by the tide, but he rode into the water, followed by his troops, and crossed in safety.[35] By the latter part of the fourteenth century the Ran was dry, for the Emperor Fīrūz Shah and his army, retreating from Sindh to Guzarāt, wandered for some days in it, and nearly perished from heat and thirst. In Kachchh an old legend attributes the drying-up of the inland sea to the curse of a holy man—a frequent and potent cause of physical changes in the East—and this and the older myth of the Mahā Bhārata (of which, however, it may be only a local modification) would seem to point to *suddenness* in the event, and no doubt as Sir A. Burnes thought, earthquakes had much to do with it. This region has suffered greatly from such catastrophes, and the earthquake of 1819 caused, as is well known, a very remarkable and extensive alteration in the surface of the Ran.

One more point may be noticed in concluding this section. It is stated by Arrian (Anab. vi. 20), that on reaching the sea by the eastern branch of the Indus, Alexander landed, and taking some cavalry with him, proceeded three marches along the coast (παρὰ θάλασσαν), and ordered wells to be dug for the watering of his fleet, it being his intention to despatch the naval expedition by the eastern and more easily navigable arm of the river. Any one who knows the nature of the Delta coast will have no hesitation in pronouncing this statement to be a fabrication. Such a march would be an utter impossibility, and the notion of wells being dug in the locality must be scouted as an absurdity. The Delta coast is so low as to be liable to inundation by high tides in ordinary weather. It is also intersected

[34] "Periplus of the Erythræan Sea," § 40.

[35] Sir H. Elliot's "History of India," vol. ii. p. 249, and appendix p. 473. The fort in which the Hindu chief took refuge is called Kandabal, Kandama, and other names. It has since been identified—I think by Colonel Watson, an excellent authority—with a place in one of the islands in the Ran.

by numberless creeks and channels, large and small, so that neither man nor horse could traverse it for any distance, and the only means of getting from point to point is by boat. But during the monsoon—the period of this alleged march—the whole sea-board is under water, and there is no part of it in which a person could travel without risk of being overwhelmed by the sea at any moment. The south-eastern corner of the Delta, too, is the most inhospitable of the whole coast. It is, in fact, a vast salt-field where life could not be maintained, and where none but poisonous water could be procured from wells if it were possible to sink them in an inundated country.[36] The episode, then, of the three days' march along the shore, and the account of the arrangement for watering the fleet must be rejected as pure fiction on the part either of Arrian or of his authority.

III.

THE DELTA ACCORDING TO LATER GREEK ACCOUNTS.

WITH the departure of Alexander and his lieutenant Nearchus from India a long period of darkness falls on the history of the Lower Indus Valley. All that we know is that when the conqueror turned his face westward there began a series of events of which the history is involved in much obscurity, but which were of deep moment to Northern India. The attempt of Alexander to incorporate the conquered Indian provinces into his Empire succeeded only so long as his presence on the scene overawed the native princes and populations. He had not yet entered on the terrible wastes of Gedrosia when the inhabitants of the Delta territory, which had been his latest acquisition, rose against his authority and expelled the Greeks from Patalene. Within the space of two years more his career was over, and the Macedonian Empire speedily fell to pieces. Among the various distributions and re-distributions of territory that followed in the course of the next few years, the Delta country seems to have fallen

[36] Some years ago an attempt was made to work the salt-field at a spot several miles from the sea. Every drop of water required by the workmen had to be brought *by boat* from a great distance.

to Porus—that prince of northern India who, after Darius, had been Alexander's most formidable opponent in his great expedition, but after defeat had been left in possession of his territory. The murder of this prince, at the instigation of one of his Greek contemporaries, and the general rising of the northern peoples headed by Chandragupta, the founder of the Maurya dynasty of Pātalīputra, followed in rapid succession. The Lower Indus Valley now became free from foreign rule, and the local chiefs were no doubt left to their own devices. Nominally the territory may have been a dependency of the Mauryan kingdom, but, separated from the main body of that kingdom by a wide expanse of desert, and at a vast distance from the capital on the Ganges, its tie of allegiance must have been of the slightest. This independence, or semi-independence, lasted under no doubt varying degrees of definiteness during the period of the Græco-Bactrian kingdom, which, though it claimed to have succeeded to Alexander's Indian conquests, had for a long time too much on its hands at home to assert its rights in India with effect, till one of its princes, Demetrius, in the second century B.C., invaded Patalene in force and completely subjected it to Bactria. His contemporary but ultimate survivor, the Græco-Indian prince, Menander, whose conquests in Northern India are said to have surpassed those of Alexander, not only held Patalene but acquired also all the territory between the Indus mouths and the mouth of the Nerbudda. Lassen ("Ind. Alt." II. 328) conjectures that Menander began to rule about 144 B.C., but H. H. Wilson ("Ariana Antiqua," p. 282) considers that the date cannot be put earlier than 126 B.C.

But while the various events above referred to were running their course, another was in progress in the distant regions of Northern China and Central Asia destined to affect the fortunes of India still more powerfully than had Greek invasions and conquests. This was the westward migration of various nomad Turanian tribes set in motion by the expulsion from the country bordering on the upper waters of the Hoangho of a tribe called *Yuë-chi*, an event which, according to Chinese historians, occurred in 165 B.C. The Yuë-chi, driven from China by the more powerful tribe of the *Hiung-nu*, or Huns, and moving north-westward to the banks of the Illi river, there came upon the numerous and martial tribe of the *Sse* whom they defeated in battle and forced to fly westward into Sogdiana, between the Iaxartes and the Oxus. Not long afterwards, however, the Yuë-chi were themselves compelled to fly in the same direction after suffering defeat at the hands of another nomad tribe, the *Usiun*, who also had been driven out of China by the masterful and restless Hiung-nu. Crossing the Iaxartes the Yuë-chi again encountered the Sse and drove them out of Sogdiana. The conquering nomads now passed through the land of the *Tawan*, that is Ferghana, defeated a people called *Tahia*, and settled for a time on the northern bank of the Oxus. It has been found possible to fix the date of this last event approximately in 124 B.C.[37] The progress of the Yuë-chi towards India was checked for a time by the opposition of the Parthians, as well as by the warlike Græco-Indian Prince, Menander, but towards the end of the last century B.C. they had reached the Indus, and early in the first century A.D. their power was fully established down to the mouths of that river. Greek writers now gave them the name of Indo-Scythians, and the Lower Indus Valley became known as Indo-Scythia. Before the arms of a lately nomad, pastoral and barbarous Turanian tribe, Greek power had everywhere succumbed in Central Asia, and had finally been extinguished in India.

All through the troublous history which has here been rapidly summarised a fact of great interest stands out prominently. This is the steady maintenance and growing importance of the foreign trade which had its outlet at the Indus mouths. From the very beginning of international maritime commerce, the Delta region, though offering special difficulties to approach by sea, must have been a point of attraction to the foreign trader. Situated at the extremity of a great natural route of traffic leading from the site of the modern Attock, at the main entrance from Central Asia to the plains of India, it was also the nearest point in the peninsula to the countries on the great Mesopotamian rivers, and to those on the shores of the Mediterranean where the commercial spirit was from the earliest ages in high activity, and maritime enterprise was energetically pursued. In the infancy of nautical adventure, when the sailor still kept within sight of land and dared not steer boldly into the open ocean, the natural course of navigation, both from the Persian Gulf and the Red Sea, would lead the trader seeking India directly to the mouths of the

[37] But the date of the complete overthrow of the Bactrian Monarchy by the Scythians, of whom the Yuë-chi were the principal tribe, is by some put at 130, by others at 126 B.C., whereas this event must have been later than the establishment of the Yuë-chi to the north of the Oxus. The date in the text is that adopted by Lassen. The chronology of all these events is involved in obscurity.

Indus. It cannot accordingly be doubted that from times far beyond the birth of history, the Chaldæan traders, who are known to have addicted themselves to mercantile enterprise by sea, were in the habit of visiting the Indus ports.[38] Merchants from Egypt and Arabia must in like manner have had their first dealings with India through the same ports, and it is likely enough that the "navy of Solomon" visited the mouths of the Indus, though we need not accept Lassen's confident assertion that *Ophir* was on that river.[39] The expedition of Alexander, by imparting a wider knowledge of the East to the western world, did much to stimulate commercial intercourse with India. This intercourse was encouraged by the Ptolemies, whose policy made Alexandria the great mart of the Mediterranean for the products of Asia. During their time the merchant vessels of Egypt, Persia and India usually met in one or other of the Sabæan ports of Arabia, whence, after the exchange of their cargoes, they returned home. Agatharchides, a Greek writer of the second century B.C., who collected his information in Alexandria, describes this trade as it existed in his day, and states that of the vessels from other parts of Asia which frequented these Arabian ports the greater number came from *Potana*, the emporium which, he says, Alexander founded at the Indus mouths. There can be no doubt as to the place referred to,

[38] Professor Sayce says, referring to a period about 4000 B.C., "We may infer that Chaldæan traders had also made their way to the western coast of India. Apart from the existence of teak in the ruins of Mugheir (ancient "Ur of the Chaldees") an ancient Babylonian list of clothing mentions *sindhu*, or muslin, the *sadin* of the Old Testament, the *σινδών* of the Greeks. That σινδών is merely "the Indian" cloth has long been recognised." (Hibbert Lectures, 1887, pp. 137, 138.) It is permissible to conjecture that this muslin got its name from the river the parts of which were of all in India the nearest, and must have been the most familiar, to Chaldæans, though of course *sindhu* may have meant anything "Indian," no matter whence imported.

[39] Lassen was greatly impressed by the resemblance between the names *Ophir* and *Abhira* ("Eine grössere Uebereinstimmung scheint nicht Bedürfniss zu seyn"); and certainly if such resemblances could be greatly relied upon in determining questions of identity, Abhīra might hold its own with *Supārā*, north of Bombay, near the mouth of the Bassein River, and the African *Sofala* which are its principal rivals. Abhīra, however, is at once put out of court by the fact that, contrary to Lassen's statement, the tribe of that name and their district, called by Ptolemy 'Αβιρια, were not located about the actual Indus mouths, but much farther inland; "*above* Patalene," says Ptolemy, that is, quite outside of the Delta. It is not improbable that, as some think, the Ophir of the O.T. is a slight alteration of a name by which the writers knew India, for the Septuagint in their version made it *Sophir*, said to be the Coptic name for India, and as that version, or most of it, was made in Egypt, there is much likelihood that the authors had no doubt Ophir meant India—not a particular port in that country, or any other.

though the writer (or perhaps his transcriber) made a little slip in the name, and was in ignorance of the fact that Alexander had only fortified and made a naval station of Patala, not founded it.[40] It must not be supposed, however, that merchant ships ever proceeded so high up the river as Patala. For keeled and sea-going vessels that would have been an impossibility. A distance, measured in a straight line from the actual seashore, of thirty miles may be taken as the probable limit of navigation for such vessels in the Indus. We must therefore assume that when Patala is mentioned as a port for foreign traders the actual fact was that cargoes from countries beyond sea reached that place by river boats, transhipment taking place at some point many miles lower down in the Delta. This method of dealing with the sea-borne traffic has indeed been a necessity in all ages and continues to be so at the present day. At this period, then, the Delta port must have been the great gathering place of the vessels which bore the varied produce of India from the ports along the western coast, and of those coming from the Red Sea and Persian Gulf to effect an exchange of cargoes; and this position it seems to have retained till some period in the first century A.D., when it lost its pre-eminence through an event of the highest importance affecting the art of navigation as then practised.

Somewhere about the middle of that century a navigator named Hippalus, whether a Greek or a Roman seems uncertain,[41] was led by his no doubt long observation of the regularity of the monsoon winds, to venture on the experiment of committing his vessel to their guidance in the open ocean. Accordingly, abandoning the hitherto universal practice of coasting, and availing himself of the south-west monsoon, he ran out to sea from the southern shores of Arabia and headed due east towards the coast of India. Happily accomplishing his object, he awaited the setting-in of the north-east monsoon, and, favoured by this, he again struck boldly across the ocean and reached an Arabian port in safety. The success of an experiment which effected an immense reduction in the period occupied by voyages between the West and India, at once brought about a revolution in the navigation of the Indian Ocean; and before the close of the century the example of the intrepid

[40] See the abstracts of the lost work of Agatharchides, as made by Photius and Diodorus (that of the latter especially) in Müller's "Geog. Græc. Minora," I. p. 191.

[41] Mr. Bunbury ("Hist. Ant. Geog." II., 351) infers from his name that he was a Greek. On the other hand M. Reinaud ("Relation des Voyages," I. xxx.) states he was a Roman. The precise period of his experimental voyage is unknown.

Hippalus was largely followed by traders to the East. The inevitable consequence was that Barygaza and the ports, on the Malabar coast, of Muziris and Nelkynda, which were in closer proximity to the more productive regions of India, began to supplant the old haven at the Indus mouths. The former, indeed, possessed another advantage over the port of Patalene, not less important than that just mentioned, in being far easier of access; for the low Delta coast, presenting no landmark for the guidance of the sailor, visible only from a very short distance, and fringed with a broad belt of shoal and sandbank, is specially difficult of approach, and dangerous to the navigator.

To the period at which we have now arrived belongs the description of the Delta, presented to us in the "Periplus of the Erythrœan Sea."[42] The information acquired by the author regarding this particular tract of country seems to have been far from extensive; but as it was almost certainly the result of personal observation and inquiry while visiting the coast, it possesses the highest interest and value. To the Lower Indus Valley he gives the name of Scythia, though at this time, according to him, Parthian invaders had contrived to subvert Indo-Scythian domination, and, albeit at variance among themselves, to establish their rule in the country. A curious fact is that the Greek-writing author never once mentions the name Patala or Patalene, and we are left to infer that the Delta capital of old times was now either no longer in existence or no longer of any importance. A new capital had taken the place of the ancient Patala, and now we have the fact of there being an actual seaport of the Delta mentioned, and a name given to it. That in the rapid succession of Græco-Bactrian, Græco-Indian, and Indo-Scythian invasions, the capital of Patalene should have succumbed would be no matter of surprise—would be indeed almost to be expected. But it is no less probable that the place fell to ruin, or at all events lost its position of importance, in consequence of changes in the course of the river, a calamity which has brought about the end of numberless towns on the Indus and other rivers of similar character. There is even some indirect evidence pointing to such a conclusion which it may be worth while to consider.

[42] There can be no doubt that the "Periplus" was *written* in the last quarter of the first century A.D. (C. Müller's "Geog. Græc. Min." I. Proleg. § 168), but the author probably made his voyages a good deal earlier, and on the whole it is perhaps safe to assume that he visited India at various times between 65 and 75 or 80 A.D.

Whereas those of Alexander's companions who described the Delta country, represented the Indus as falling into the sea by only two mouths, and these, as we have seen, were evidently on the extreme eastern and western limits of the Delta, the "Periplus" states that the river had seven mouths, "but these are narrow and full of shallows, and all except the middle one are unnavigable."[43] Through this middle mouth then the bulk of the river water must at this time have been forcing its way to the sea. The two great branches explored by Alexander, the western of which had borne the fleet of Nearchus to the sea, had now dried up; or rather, to use the expression in the "Periplus," the accuracy of which will be recognised by those who have seen the old river channels, the water in them was stagnant and lying in pools (τεναγώδη). Now, remembering the law which governs the lateral movements of the river, it is evident that the change of embouchure from the borders to the centre of the Delta must have been accompanied—indeed, occasioned—by considerable shiftings of the bed higher upstream. As, then, the river-bed in the upper country moved westwards so the western arm in the Lower Delta (Nearchus' Channel) would be abandoned by the water, which would seek an outlet farther east;—the stream, in straightening its course, would push its mouth towards the middle of the Delta. But the effect of this westward movement of the channel in the upper country would be to make it break away from the eastward flowing branch (of Alexander's time) which would then dry up. This process might be gradual, that is through the erosion of the western bank, or sudden, that is by the bursting of the river into an entirely new course, as happened last century north of Ḫaydarābād, but in the end the stream would run into one channel only, producing the state of things described in the "Periplus." These shiftings of the river have been going on through all ages, and evidence of the fact may be seen in the number of dried-up eastward running channels, many of them now in fragments, which score the face of the Delta region, as well as of the country to the north of it.[44]

[43] "Periplus," § 38.

[44] It is perhaps open to question whether the Indus in Alexander's time ran into the sea by two mouths *all the year round.* The statement in Arrian, indeed (Anab. VI., 18), that near Patala the Indus divided into two *large* rivers, and that both *retained the name Indus* down to the sea, would seem to indicate that both carried water perennially. It must be remembered, however, that the Greeks were in

Thus the movement of the river bed to the westward in the upper country would take it away from Patala, which would then be disconnected from its seaport, and even if it remained habitable would no longer retain its position as an emporium of foreign trade. Whatever the explanation, the fact of the disappearance of Patala as a place of any note by the second half of the first century seems unquestionable. That the name finds a place in Ptolemy's Geography, written more than half a century later than the date of the "Periplus," is easily accounted for when it is considered that Ptolemy must have collected his immense mass of place-names from many writers old and recent, and that he no doubt simply added the information obtained by travellers of later times to that which he found recorded by writers on Alexander's Expedition, without inquiry as to how far the older accounts were in conformity with existing circumstances.

According to the author of the "Periplus" the Delta seaport of his time was named Barbarikon, and was situated on the middle mouth of the river, having a small island in front of it.[45] It must not be supposed that the port was on, or close to, the actual coast, for in such a situation it would have been liable to destruction by high tides, or by storm-waves from the Indian Ocean. Like all the Delta

Patalene only during the season of high flood, when of course they would find both branches flowing full to the sea. It may well have been, however, that but one of these was perennial while the other was merely a flood-channel, becoming dry, or nearly dry, during the low season. So far as I know there is no evidence, whether from the observation of Europeans in modern times, or from the records of past centuries, to show that the river has ever discharged any very considerable proportion of its waters into the sea by more than one mouth throughout the entire year. The *Rēn* (see above, p. 4) may have been perennial, though there are some facts which seem to tell against that supposition; but, as the remains of its course still show, it was insignificant in size compared with the main stream. Bearing in mind the constant westward tendency of the river's lateral movement, I should conjecture that the western branch of Alexander's time was in reality the main channel, and that the eastern branch carried a large body of water during the flood-season only. Some confirmation of this conjecture may be found in the fact that Alexander appears to have found the eastern more easily navigable than the western branch,* which may be explained by the supposition that the former contained a smaller volume of water and had a much less violent current than the latter. The remarks above made would not always apply in the case of the lower Delta (below Ṭhaṭa) where sometimes branch channels of considerable size are in activity throughout the year.

* This may perhaps be inferred from the absence of any mention of difficulties or disasters such as were encountered in the voyage down the western branch. No statement is made on the subject; it is only said that the navigation of the *mouth* of the stream was easier than that of the western branch.

[45] "Periplus," § 38.

ports of which we have any knowledge, Barbarikon would no doubt be some distance up the river, and probably not less than ten to fifteen miles—the minimum distance from the sea for safety. The small island would be one of the numerous tracts of land in the Delta which are isolated by minor branch channels. Being somewhere about the middle of the lower Delta, the port was perhaps not far from the position of the modern *Shāh Bandar* (see Map III.); and, contrary to the opinion of Sir H. Elliot and General Cunningham, must certainly not be identified with Bhambhor on the Ghāro,[46] a place on the north-western border of the Delta. The latter writer founds his identification on the supposition that Bhambhor was accessible from the middle mouth of the Indus, but, whether it was or not, it is said in the "Periplus" that Barbarikon was actually *on* (ἐπὶ οὗ), not merely to be reached from, the middle mouth. Barbarikon is, of course, a corruption, and it would be idle to seek to identify it with names of comparatively modern date.

The capital of the so-called Scythia is named *Minnagara*, and described as lying behind Barbarikon and inland, but how far inland is not stated. It is said that the sea-going vessels came to anchor at Barbarikon, and that the entire cargoes were then taken by river (in river craft is evidently implied) to the king at the metropolis. This latter fact would seem to show that Minnagara was at no great distance from the seaport in the Delta. It is at least difficult to believe that such an arrangement would be enforced if the capital were at the spot where Lassen (in his map accompanying the "Indische Alterthumskunde") places it, namely thirty miles north of Sēwaṉ, which would sometimes take six weeks to reach from a Delta port. In thus determining its site he seems to have been guided by Ptolemy's purely fanciful latitudes and longitudes, which, it is clear, could only serve to mislead. General Cunningham places the metropolis at Ṭhaṭa, which, having been for long the chief town of the Delta, has been made to do much service in the cause of dubious identifications. That Minnagara was somewhere in or near the latitude of Ṭhaṭa is probable enough, but General Cunningham's reasons for identifying it with Ṭhaṭa can easily be shown to be fallacious. He considers, in the first place, that Ṭhaṭa is the Manjābarī of the Arab geographers, then that for Manjābarī it is permissible to read Mandābarī, then that

[46] See Elliot, "Hist. of India," I. App. p. 368; and Cunningham, "Anc. Geog. India," p. 294.

Mands and Mins were the same, and thus he comes to the conclusion that Manjābarī, Minnagara, and Ṭhaṭa are identical. But in identifying Manjābarī with Ṭhaṭa General Cunningham is clearly in error, as will be proved in another section relating to a much later period. There is, in fact, no possibility of making even a plausible guess at the position of Minnagara, owing to the vagueness of the "Periplus" in the matter, and we must be content to leave the question in the obscurity in which it has been handed down to us in consequence of a probably accidental oversight on the part of the author.[47]

We may now pass on to the next account of the Delta;—that which we find in the Geography of Ptolemy. This brings us down to about the middle of the second century of our era. The information to be extracted from Ptolemy leaves much to be desired in point of exactness, a defect which is not compensated by his copious lists of names of places which cannot now be identified, accompanied by statements of latitude and longitude possessing no value whatever. He says the Lower Indus Valley is commonly called *Indo-Scythia*, and describes it as divided into Patalene, or the Delta region, and Abiria, a district "situated above" Patalene. He follows or confirms the statement of the "Periplus" that the Indus had seven mouths, the names of which he gives (Lib. vii. cap. i. sec. 2).

1. The most westerly mouth of the Indus, called Sagapa.
2. The next mouth of the Indus, called Sinthon.
3. The third, which is called Chrysoun.
4. The fourth ,, Chariphron.
5. The fifth ,, Sapara.
6. The sixth ,, Sabalaessa.
7. The seventh ,, Lonibare.

No one of these is to be recognised in any of the modern names of the Indus mouths. It would be surprising indeed were it otherwise, considering that the Lower Delta channels are constantly changing, that old mouths and their names disappear and give place to new,

[47] Just before coming to his account of Scythia, the author, in describing a portion of the country on the coast of what he calls the Gulf of Gedrosia (including, perhaps, Son Miāṉī Bay), uses precisely the same phrase as that which refers to Minnagar, in stating the position of the town of Parsis relatively to that of the small port of Oraia, namely, κατα νώτου μεσόγειος, but adding, "distant seven days journey from the sea." The omission of a like defining clause in the case of Minnagara was no doubt a mere slip on the author's part. The local history named Tuhfatu'l-Kirām mentions a *Min-nagar* as having formerly existed in Pargana Shahdādpur. If this was the Parthian capital its site must have been on the Luhāno channel, and we should have proof that the Indus was running in that channel in the first century A.D., in which case it would be a reasonable inference that it was probably so running in Alexander's time.

and that probably those belonging to one century are forgotten in the next. But the Sagapa and the Lonibare, from the positions assigned to them as the farthest west and the farthest east respectively, may be identified with the present Ghāro and Korī channels. Ghāro, or Ghārā, is a Sindhī word meaning a "creek," and it has no doubt been substituted for an older name since the western channel lost its connection with the Indus and became a mere tidal creek. Sinthon, of course, represents *Sindhu*, the Aryan name of the river. Lonibare is a name that may, I think, be accounted for, and it raises a physiographical question of some interest. Lassen (I.A. I. 97, n. 2) quotes the geographer Ritter as an authority for the statement that the Purān was formerly called Lūnī, and suggests that the Lonibare mouth owed its name to this circumstance. I believe, however, that Ritter was quite mistaken, and that he confounded the Purān with the Lūnī, or Lonī (properly Lawanī = "saline"), a river of Rājputānā, with a course of some two hundred miles, and running into the Ran at its north-east corner. "B̠ārī" is an old Sindhī suffix to place-names, of which we have examples in *Ghorāb̠ārī*, a place on the Ghorā channel in the middle of the Lower Delta, and in *Hurb̠āri*, a township in the Shahdādpur Pargana in Central Sindh. Lonibare may well then have meant the channel through which the Lonī finally reached the sea. If so, the course of that river must have then been continuous diagonally through the Ran from N.E. to S.W., whereas now it has hardly any course traceable in the Ran, its water merely spreading over the surface of that depression for a short distance, and being quickly absorbed by the sand. The rise of the surface of the Ran which we know to have taken place would account for the disappearance of the bed of the Lonī in it, but it may also be the case that, from some cause unknown to us, the volume of that river may now be less than it was in the remote times referred to.

Among the towns mentioned by Ptolemy as situated on the Indus we find *Binagara*, which may be a copyist's mistake for Minnagara. No indication of its position is given beyond the inclusion of it among those stated to be by the river and on the eastern bank, and also the delusive latitude and longitude. Patala and Barbarei (of course the Barbarikon of the "Periplus") are described as "in the islands formed by the river," meaning "in the Delta," but how far from the sea is not said. Ptolemy, in mentioning Patala, evidently follows the writers on Alexander's Expedition, though when he wrote his geography the river, as has been shown, must have moved some distance from its position in Alexander's time, and the old capital of the Delta was probably no longer in existence.

NOTE.—Some further reference to one or two of Ptolemy's names of the Indus mouths will be found in a later portion of this memoir.

IV.

THE DELTA ACCORDING TO THE ACCOUNTS OF EARLY EASTERN WRITERS.

STILL descending the stream of time, we find the next accounts of the Indus Valley in the sixth and seventh centuries; and now we begin to draw our information from the works of Eastern writers. From this time a large but occasionally varying extent of territory on the Indus is known only by its old name of Sindh, from the Aryan name of the river.

The work which comes first in order of time is that of a Chinese author, the Buddhist monk Hiuen Tsang, whose *Si-yu-ki*, or "Records of the Western World," made known to Europe through the translation of M. Stanislas Julien, and more recently through that of the late Professor Beal,[48] contains an account of his travels in India in the period 629-645 A.D. Towards the close of this period he visited some part of Sindh, and it is thought by some of his modern commentators that he passed through the Delta country—an opinion which I formerly shared, but which a further study of the Si-yu-ki since Professor Beal's translation appeared has led me to alter.

The account of Sindh is one of the disappointing portions of the Si-yu-ki. Hiuen Tsang's Sindh, in fact, is not the Sindh of any period known to history, and his description of it is wholly irreconcilable with the facts which we gather from the contemporary history embodied in the work which is next to come under notice (the "Tārīkh-i-Hind wa Sind"). He places the capital on the west of the

[48] "Si-yu-ki—Buddist Records of the Western World." Translated from the Chinese of Hiuen Tsiang, by Samuel Beal, B.A. Trübner, 1884. 2 vols. It is always to Professor Beal's translation that reference is made in this memoir, but I follow Professor Terrien de Lacouperie in writing Hiuen *Tsang*, instead of Hiuen *Tsiang* (*Journ. R. A. S.*, October 1892.)

Indus, whereas we know it was on the east bank, its ruins and the long dried-up channel of the river being still to be seen in attestation of the fact. He calls it P'i-shen-p'o-pu-lo, which Chinese scholars take to represent such names as Vichavapur, or Vasmapur, or Balmapur; and General Cunningham, taking rather an unwarrantable liberty with the Chinese syllables, turns into Abhijānwapur.[49] All these names, unknown in Sindh and unmentioned in its histories, serve only to mystify us, and the case becomes worse when Hiuen Tsang says that Multan was only "900 li or so"—that is, some 150 miles—distant from the capital of Sindh, and to the *east* of it, the fact being that Multan was 250 miles from it and north-east of it. To all of this must be added his statement that the king was a Shudra (Shu-t'o-lo), while from the source above-mentioned we learn that at this time (about 641 A.D.) a Brahman ruled Sindh. Some clue is obtained to the country which the Buddhist monk had in his mind when he spoke of Sindh from his remark that: "They find here a great quantity of salt which is *red* like cinnabar; also white salt, black salt, and *rock*-salt." (Si-yu-ki II. 272). It is clear from this that the Sindh of Hiuen Tsang included the *Salt Range*, since nowhere else lower down the Indus could rock-salt be found. The northern limits of Sindh have sometimes extended to that range; and at the time when Hiuen Tsang was travelling in this part of India, Multan and a considerable district around it had recently been reconquered from revolted chiefs, and had been incorporated in the dominions of the Brahman Chaeh, Prince of Sindh, whose capital was at Alor. Such is the statement of the "Tārīkh-i-Hind wa Sind." P'i-shen-p'o-pu-lo must therefore be looked for somewhere in the Dērajāt. It could not possibly have been 150 miles *west* of Multan, for if it had been we should have to seek for it to the west of the Sulaymān Range; and the probability is that Hiuen Tsang made a mistake in his bearings, as he certainly did on other occasions, and that he ought to have said "south" when he said "east."[50]

[49] There is a village named Abhijāno, a little to the south of the old capital, which suggested this restoration to General Cunningham. He says Abhijan is Sanscrit for "fame," "and is not improbably connected with Hwen Thsang's Pi-shen-po-pu-lo." ("An. Geog.," p. 259.) The connection seems to leave something to be desired in the way of explanation.

[50] A legitimate restoration of the Chinese symbols would, I think, be *Vaishnavapur* = "City of the followers of Vishnu," but whether a town of that name ever existed in the Dērajāt I have no idea. As for Alor, Hiuen Tsang would certainly have called that town *O-lo-lo*, and would not have gone out of his way in search of some antiquated and fanciful appellation.

The question of Hiuen Tsang having visited Lower Sindh is complicated with that of the identification of the country he calls 'O-tin-p'o-chi-lo, restored by Professor Beal, without note or comment, to Atyanabakēla, a name hitherto unheard of. The professor was in fact obliged to abstain from explanation, having compromised himself by a previous unfortunate attempt at identification. Hiuen Tsang, after visiting Malwa, proceeded to the country of K'ie-ch'a, distant 300 li, or fifty miles. This country Professor Beal identifies with Kac̱hc̱hha, though he admits that Kheḍa "is the equivalent of K'ie-ch'a." He says that Kheḍa (called by the English, who detest a palatal *d*, Kaira) is the name of a town, but K'ie-ch'a was the name of a country, and on this ground, and the still more extraordinary one of *distance*, he determines that K'ie-ch'a meant Kac̱hc̱hha. But he is undoubtedly wrong. Kheḍa is the name of a very ancient province or tract of country in Guzerat, as well as of the chief town in that tract, and some part of its eastern border may perhaps have been distant from the Malwa frontier what might roughly be called fifty miles (it is now, when Kheḍa is a British district, much less). The fact that Kac̱hc̱hha is 1200 li from the western frontier of Malwa was not considered by the Professor, or, if it was, it did not stagger him. The want of local knowledge, too, prevented him from seeing that there were other facts equally conclusive against his identification. Hiuen Tsang says: "The population (of K'ie-ch'a) is dense; the establishments wealthy (meaning that the families are well off); the country is an appanage of Mālava; and the climate, products of the soil and manners of the people are very similar in both countries"; and of Malwa he says: "The soil is rich and fertile and produces abundant harvests." K'ie-ch'a, then, was densely populated and very fertile, and so the Kheḍa country is at this day; but to affirm such things of Kac̱hc̱hha in any age would have been ridiculous, and in fact we find that Hiuen Tsang gave a very different account of that province, and one that is quite in accordance with the state of things now existing. For there cannot be a shadow of doubt that 'O-tin-p'o-chi-lo—inexplicable, like the name of the Sindh capital—meant Kac̱hc̱hha. "The chief town is Khie-tsi-shi-fa-lo (certainly Kotishwara, long since contracted to Koteshwar and Kotesar.[51] "*It*

[51] Kotishwara (= "ten million gods") is most probably the place which appears in translations of El Birūnī's work on India as *Tawalleshar*. In the Arabic text in M. Reinaud's "Fragments" (p. 91), the name is written تولّيشر, but I suspect that

lies on the river Sindh and borders on the ocean," and I may add that it still contains a temple of Maheshvara where the "Pāshupata heretics" worship just as in the days of the Chinese pilgrim. Again: "Lately there has been no ruler; it (the province) is under the protection of Sindh. The soil is *low and damp*, and the ground is impregnated with salt. It is covered with wild shrubs, and is mostly waste land." (Si-yu-ki, II. 276). Here we have Ka<u>ch</u><u>ch</u>ha exactly described. Its very name is unconsciously explained by Hiuen Tsang, for it is due to the circumstance of its surface being "low and damp." It is surprising that Professor Beal could miss the identification.

Hiuen Tsang now proceeds: "On leaving the kingdom of O-tin-p'o-chi-lo, and going north 700 li or so, we come to the country of Pi-to-shi-lo." Professor Beal gives *Pitāshilā* as an equivalent of this name, and General Cunningham thinks that this stands for Patala, which he identifies with <u>H</u>aydarābād. Now 700 li, or 117 miles, is almost exactly the distance from Kotesar to <u>H</u>aydarābād, and, the direction from the former is nearly north, but other considerations point to the conclusion that the country meant by Pi-to-shi-lo lay much further east. It is the custom of the pilgrim when a journey takes him across a large river to mention the fact. Thus he mentions the crossing of the Ganges and Nerbudda, the crossing and re-crossing of the Indus on entering, and on leaving, Sindh. It is, then, natural to expect that if he crossed the Indus to reach Pi-to-shi-lo we should have that fact recorded, and he could not possibly in those days have arrived at the position of <u>H</u>aydarābād without crossing the river. He might even have been obliged to cross the Korī creek as well as the main river, and that would perhaps have been a matter of hours.[52] As, then, there is not a word to indicate that the Indus had to be crossed in the journey to Pi-to-shi-lo, it seems to be a fair presumption that the country so named was on the same side of the river as O-tin-p'o-chi-lo, that is, to

we have here one of those corruptions to which the Arabic alphabet lends itself with such fatal facility. At all events it is easy to see how well the original text may have had کوتیسر. Tawalleshar is mentioned by El Birūnī next after Dēbal, and as being fifty farsakhs from that place, which *by water* would suit fairly well for Kotēsar. No such place as Tawalleshar is known. Both Koṭēsar and the neighbouring Nārāyansar (Nārāyansarowar) are extremely ancient.

[52] It took Mr. Eastwick, in 1839, a whole day to cross from Lakhpat to the usual landing-place in Sindh. (See his "Dry Leaves from Young Egypt.") The tedious transit is unavoidable, as it is necessary to sail some distance up the creek.

the east of it. Where, then, was it? The distance is said to be 700 li, but the precise point of departure, according to the vexatious habit of the pilgrim, is not named, and it becomes increasingly difficult to conjecture where to look for Pi-to-shi-lo.[53] As regards Hiuen Tsang's distances, we find these invariably stated in round numbers—in so many *hundreds* (or thousands) of *li*, but we must not imagine that he was in the habit of calculating the length of journeys, frequently of very long duration, in terms of a standard falling short of 300 yards. No doubt the actual standard was the universal one in olden times of "a day's journey," and with the Chinese this was probably taken as roughly averaging the convenient number of 100 li (about sixteen English miles).[54] We may then take it that in the present case the distance was 7 days' journey "*or so*," for this expression is almost always used by Hiuen Tsang, and, of course, in order to convey that his estimates have no pretension to anything like precision. But in some journeys the average of the "day" might be greatly exceeded—might even be doubled—as, for instance, in tracts of country where water was very scarce, and where on this account it might be necessary to travel very long distances without halting; and yet, in stating the distance in *li*, mere habit or forgetfulness might cause the ordinary average to be taken as the basis of reckoning. Such is very likely to have been the case in regard to this particular journey, for whatever direction the pilgrim took he must needs have passed through a wide tract of nearly desert land. With respect to the real equivalent of Pi-to-shi-lo, I have no doubt whatever that Pitāshilā is a mistake. The Chinese syllables might equally represent such names as Bēdāsīr and Pītāsīr,[55] and the termination *sīr* or *sar*, is very common in place-names in Mārwār, and is not uncommon in that portion of eastern Sindh situated between Umarkot and the Ran of Kachchh, called *Dhāt*, which has

[53] This was the name of some district, and apparently also of its chief town, for the "capital" is referred to but not named.

[54] Thus we find that a distance which Hiuen Tsang calls 300 li is called by his fellow-countryman and biographer Hwui-lih, "three days journey." (Si-yu-ki II. 265, n.)

[55] These equivalents were suggested by Professor Beal himself when reading a paper at a meeting of the Royal Asiatic Society at which I was present, but in a letter subsequently written to me, he informed me that he was not disposed to adhere to them, entirely, I believe, on the ground that no place with a name resembling them was known in Sindh. I cannot help thinking this unfortunate, and that further research might lead to the discovery that in his suggested restorations he had struck upon the truth, or, at all events, had come near it.

for ages belonged ethnically to Mārwār, and was long politically connected with that province. It is here perhaps that we ought to look for whatever district our pilgrim meant by Pi-to-shi-lo, and I would suggest that the Nagar Pārkar country, which contains some very ancient remains, might be what we are in search of;[56] or, again, the district about Ūmarkot (anciently called Amarkot), or that immediately to the west of it, in the Mīrpur Khās Pargana, or a little south of it. This last portion of Eastern Sindh is certainly more likely to have contained a "dense population," as we are told Pi-to-shi-lo did, than any part of the Dhāt country.

From Pi-to-shi-lo Hiuen Tsang proceeded to 'O-fan-ch'a, distant "300 li or so," and in a north-easterly direction. The equivalent of this name is given as *Awanda*, but with a note of doubt attached to it. This, I believe, is quite unknown. It would seem to have been somewhere in the Khairpur territory. General Cunningham identifies the unnamed capital of 'O-fan-ch'a with the ancient city of Brahmanābād, but I think for very insufficient reasons. What is certain is that this district, like the other two previously mentioned, was a dependency of Sindh. Of each of the three it is said that it had "no chief ruler," but was subject to Sindh. That this was true of Kachchha some seventy years later than the pilgrim's time we learn incidentally from the account of the Arab conquest of Sindh in the "Tārīkh-i-Hind wa Sind." Here we may take leave of the pilgrim. The probability is that for some reason or other—perhaps the unsettled state of the country lying nearer to the Indus in consequence of the recent extinction of an old dynasty, and the succession to the throne of an usurper and an upstart—facts which are on record—he kept on the outskirts of Sindh, and purposely avoided the large towns, such as Brahmanābād, in the neighbourhood of the river. That he was ever anywhere near the position of the present Ḥaydarābād is extremely improbable. It is inconceivable that he should go out of his way merely to visit an insignificant outlying stronghold like *Nīrūn*, which we know then occupied the

[56] A few miles north-east of the town of Nagar Parkar is a place called Pītāpur = "town of Pītā," a name which suggests that there may very well have been a Pītāsīr in Dhāt in earlier times. There is a Būdāsir in Mārwār, but of comparatively modern origin, and much too distant to allow of its being thought of in the present connection. These names are mentioned merely to show that Professor Beal's abandoned restorations were at least quite in accordance with known place-nomenclature, while Pitāshilā is not.

site on which the fort of Ḫaydarābād was built last century. It would have been interesting if we could have traced his route along the countries on the Indus with some degree of certainty, but his fancies, or his errors, in the matter of place-names have rendered that impossible.

We now turn to slightly later, but much more detailed and satisfactory sources of information in the works of early Muhammedan writers.

The curious, and, for many reasons, deeply interesting old local chronicle, known as the *Tārīkh-i-Hind wa Sind*, and also as the *Chach Nāma*, contains an account of the earliest Muhammedan enterprises in India in the aggressions by the Arabs on the Sindh frontiers in the latter part of the seventh century A.D., and their ultimate conquest of all the territory between Multān and the mouths of the Indus in the beginning of the next century. It is a Persian version made, in the early part of the thirteenth century, by one Muhammed 'Ali (a native of Kūfa in 'Irāq, who had emigrated from his country and settled in Uchh), of an Arabic original drawn up apparently soon after the conquest of Sindh by one who took part in that event. The earlier portion of the work treats of Sindh when it was ruled by Hindu princes long before the Muhammedan invasion, or even the rise of Islām, and takes us back to the latter half of the sixth century. This part of the chronicle is no doubt merely an embodiment of the local traditions current in the country about the time of the conquest.[57] These have received, as was inevitable, a colouring distinctly due to Muhammedan fancy, but there seems to be no reason to doubt that they contain on the whole a considerable amount of historical truth. The account of the relations between Sindh and Arabia in the early years of Islām, and the narrative of the invasion and conquest are told with much simplicity, the reverses and misfortunes of the Muhammedans being recorded no less than their triumphs. The style of the Persian translation is, as stated by

[57] Sindh was the refuge of various Arab rebels and outlaws for several years before the conquest. Among these was the family of the *'Ilāfiyy*, one of whom held a high position at the court of the Sindhian prince Rāe Dāhir, and is frequently mentioned in the Chach Nāma. From this we learn that after the conquest he was pardoned (he had refused to fight against Muslims), and it is probable that from him the author of the Arabic original of that chronicle received most of the information relating to the period preceding the Arab invasion.

Sir H. Elliot, for the most part plain and unaffected, but the text, in the only two copies which I have seen, is in many places corrupt, with the result of producing much confusion, and rendering many passages absolutely unintelligible. The work is somewhat marred, too, by inconsistencies and contradictions, which seem to have been occasioned by various authorities not in agreement with one another having been drawn upon for some of the matter recorded. With all its defects, however, the Chach Nāma remains a work of great value as a translation of one of the earliest histories by an Arab writer, and as a record of the first conquest effected by Muhammedan arms in India.[58] Of this event so glorious for Islām only one other detailed account by an Arab historian is extant. This is found in the work entitled "*Kitāb Futūhu'l Buldān*," or Book of the Conquests of Countries, written by Ahmed, son of Yahya, surnamed El Biladhurī, in the second half of the ninth century of our era. A chapter of this work, headed "*Futūhu's-Sind*" (Conquests of Sind), is devoted to a narrative of the various raids into Sindh led by the Arab chiefs who were in command on its western frontiers, of the final conquest of the country, and of the events which occurred there under the governors

[58] A complete and very appreciative account of the "Chach Nāma" will be found in the first volume of Sir H. Elliot's "History of India," preceding the translated extracts from the chronicle. In regard to these extracts it is to be regretted that there has been some want of judgment in their selection. Some might have been omitted with advantage, and there might have been a larger admission of portions of the narrative descriptive of the actual campaign. It was not a happy circumstance, too, that the gentleman selected to edit Elliot's "History," however competent in other respects, had no personal knowledge of India, and was consequently unable to comment on or explain several matters demanding local knowledge for their satisfactory treatment. The suspicion entertained by many of the genuineness and authenticity of the Chach Nāma, due to the fact of its containing some clearly legendary matter mixed up with what purports to be history, has caused the work to be neglected; but after an attentive study of it, and after translating a considerable portion of it, I am happy to find myself in agreement with so high an authority as Sir H. Elliott in believing it to be genuine, and to give in the main a trustworthy account of one of the most interesting events in the history of India—the first collision between the Semite and the Aryan in that country. The defects of the existing text are easily accounted for by the number of transcripts of which it is the latest result. The author's manuscript must have been in the Kufic character, no other being then known to Arabs, and doubtless its contents had been copied and recopied in neo-Arabic when, 500 years later, Muhammed 'Ali discovered the work at Bakhar in the possession of a descendant of the author. The correspondence purporting to have been carried on between Hajjāj, the celebrated Governor of 'Irāq, and his young relative Muhammed Qāsim, who commanded the Sindh Expedition, may be regarded as imaginary. To accept it as genuine would be to presuppose a despatch-writing and despatch-preserving Army Staff with which we can hardly credit the military organisation of those times.

appointed by the Khalīfas down nearly to the period when Bilādhurī wrote. The Futūhu's-Sind is closely in agreement with the Chach Nāma in regard to the main current of the events recorded, but it enters far less into detail than the latter, and is in fact a simple and almost prosaic narrative strongly suggestive of truthfulness. The exact accord frequently noticeable between the two authors naturally induces the impression of their having drawn from a common source, and in one or two instances they do cite the same authority; but a careful study of both works will confirm the belief that they were composed independently, and that their many points of agreement may be regarded as evidence of the general trustworthiness of the history which they relate.

From the Chach Nāma we learn that in the sixth century A.D. the port of the Delta was named *Dēbal,* the Arabic modification of the Indian word *Dēwal,* a temple; for the place, we are told, contained a temple which appears to have enjoyed some celebrity. The actual site of this port is now unknown, but we learn from the Arab geographers of the tenth century that it was somewhere in the western Delta. Sir H. Elliot thinks it was at or near Karāchī, and that the temple probably stood on the headland of Manora.[59] It is certain, however, that no temple would be built on a site so inconvenient in point of access as Manora, and at a distance of fully five miles from fresh water. And he is certainly in error when, endeavouring to find further support for his location of Dēbal, he says (*l.c.*), "Bilādhurī speaks of the *Bay* of Debal," which, if it were true, would be decisive of the question, since Karāchī bay is the only bay that exists in that region. But it was not Bilādhurī but his French translator, M. Reinaud, who spoke of a "bay." The former used the expression خورآلديبل (Khawru'l Daybal) that is, the Debal *estuary or creek*, and M. Reinaud translated it "la *baie* de Daybal."[60] Dēbal, then,

[59] "History of India," I. App. p. 376. In a footnote he remarks that "the temple was contiguous to the town of Dēbal, not within it," and he refers to Bilādhurī as his authority for this statement; but Bilādhurī's words are *bi'l Daybal,* that is strictly "*in* Dēbal," though they might have been used if the temple had been outside the town but close to it. The Chach Nāma, however, is explicit, using the expression *dar miyān-i-Dēbal,* "*in*—in the midst of—Dēbal." M. Reinaud's version of the "Futūh" has, what is a correct equivalent *in French,* "*à* Daybal," and Sir Henry's translator, following this version instead of the Arabic original, rendered the expression "at" in place of "in" Dēbal.

[60] It is curious that M. Reinaud made the same mistake in translating El Birūnī's work ("Fragments," p. 119), rendering خور "*baie,*" though in this very place El

according to Bilādhurī, was clearly on one of the Delta channels, but we have no further information from him which enables us to fix its position more precisely. The Arab geographers of the tenth century are also very vague in their descriptions of its situation. In the map of Sindh in the "Ashkālu'l-Belād," which appears to have been the work of Ibnu Hawqil (Elliot, I. 32), as well as in that by Istakhrī, Dēwal is shown as lying to the west of the Indus (the main stream must be understood, no other being represented) and on the very shore of the sea. But no town could possibly exist in a situation where it would be exposed to destruction during the stormy seasons, and where such a necessary of life as fresh water would have to be brought from long distances; to say nothing of the impossibility of a port being established on the open Delta coast. All the known Delta ports have been well inland, at distances from the sea (by river) of sixteen to thirty miles or even more. The sole exception is the port of *Kētī*, established since the British conquest, which is only ten or twelve miles from the sea, and has three times been destroyed by inundations during the south-west monsoon; and Dēbal was no mere ordinary Delta port with few or no solid buildings, and consisting of a collection of huts intended for habitation only during the shipping season. It is evident that at the time of its capture by the Arabs it was a town of some size and respectably fortified. Its temple was large enough to afford a last refuge for many of the besieged, and from its recesses the victors brought forth no fewer than 700 "lovely damsels" belonging to the sacred establishment. This is probably an exaggeration, but it is allowable to regard the story as evidence that the building was of large proportions and was maintained on a grand scale.[61] We are also told that when, under special orders from 'Irāq, the town was given over to military execution, the carnage lasted for three days—a proof that its population cannot have been inconsiderable. Bilādhurī says that when the Muhammedan com-

Birūnī distinctly describes it as an *estuary*—a place where, he says, sweet water runs into and mingles with the sea—while he defines the غُبّ (ghubb), not felicitously but intelligibly enough, as being "like a bending or winding-in" of the sea on the land—that is, a bay. The northern part of Karāchī harbour might perhaps be called a "Khawr," as there the Liārī (a flood-channel, always dry except after heavy rain) runs into it, and, according to some maps, the sea at the entrance of the harbour is called "Khur 'Ali." The word *Khawr* is sometimes used in Makrān for a "river."

[61] In Colonel Tod's "Rājāsthān," there is mention of Dēwal as a *Tīrtha*, or sacred bathing-place, to which pilgrimages were made from Rājputāna.

mander got possession of the place he garrisoned it with 4,000 men. There can be no doubt, then, that a town of this size and importance would be situated far enough inland to be beyond the reach of tidal waves and floods, and as far up the channel on which it lay as could be conveniently reached by foreign vessels trading to Sindh. It would also be in a position having easy communication by land with the interior, and would not therefore be in the network of channels far down in the Delta. Its most probable situation would be somewhere on the right bank of the *Baghār* channel whence the interior could be reached without crossing, at the most, more than one stream. Now among the sites of ruined towns in the Western Delta there is one on the right bank of the Baghār, at a spot twenty miles south-west of Ṭhaṭa, which seems to me to be very probably the remains of ancient Dēwal. (See Map III.) Authentic history of these ruins there is none, but according to local tradition they are the remains of a once flourishing port, the residence of a large trading community and of State officials. The present name of the site is *Kakaṛ Bukēra,* Bukēra being the name of the township (locally called *Dēh*) in which it lies, and being also an old tribal name. Now it is mentioned in the Chach Nāma that on the occasion of a certain chief's being appointed governor of Dēwal the "Deh of *Bakrī*" was assigned to him for his maintenance. This name may very likely be a corruption, resulting from many copyings, of Bukēra, the difference between the two when written in Persian being but trifling (بکیرا and بکري); and as it would be natural—especially in those unsettled times—that the land from which the governor was to draw his revenue should be immediately round the town, it seems to be no far-fetched inference that Bukēra was the township assigned, and that the ruined site it contains is that of Dewal.[62] And this identification agrees very well with such other evidence as we can glean in regard to the position of the old port. Ibnu Khurdādba says (Elliot, I. 15) that "from Debal to the junction of the river Mihrān (Indus) with the sea is two para-

[62] Very many townships, and their names, in Sindh—as indeed throughout India—are of extreme antiquity. Towns and villages succumb to the violence of man or to natural calamity, disappear and are known no more, but usually the township with its name endures through all vicissitudes. Hence it is much safer to seek for ancient names among those of present townships than among those of existing towns or villages. How old the Bukēra township may be I cannot say, but I am informed that the Bukēra tribe, or sub-tribe, have very long been settled here and in the neighbourhood. Another name for the ruined site is *Bēg Chugyo.*

sangs," and Masudī (Ibid. p. 24) that the mouth of the Mihrān is "about 2 days' journey from the town of Dēbal." This apparent inconsistency may be explained by the supposition that the former writer wrote "parasangs" (*farsang*) when he meant "days." From what has been stated above, it is evident that Dēbal could not have been at so short a distance from the sea as 7–8 miles, and in any case Masūdī, who had himself travelled in Sindh, would be the better authority on such a point. But when he says "2 days'" journey we must understand a distance *by river* equal to 2 days' journey (roughly 40 miles), as nobody would travel between the two points by land, crossing deep channels and creeks on the way. This distance just suits the Bukēra identification, the ruins being 35 to 40 miles from the sea by the Baghār river.[63] Lastly, we have the distance between Dēbal and *Nīrūn* stated in the Chach Nāma as 25 farsakhs. The site of Nīrūn is very well known to be that of the present fort of Ḫaydarābād, the ruins of the ancient stronghold having been in existence and surrounded by a burial ground till 1763, when Ghulām Shāh Kalhorā swept all away in founding the fortress of his new capital. The value of the "farsakh" is of course a matter of uncertainty. Sir H. Elliot considered that 2½ miles might be taken as a minimum, and 3 miles as a maximum, equivalent of that vague standard. But looking to the authorities cited by himself (I. App. p. 400 *n.*) it would seem that a *minimum* of 3 miles would be a safer value to assume. The real fact is that though a definite value has at different times been assigned to the farsakh, in practical use its value has varied among different peoples according to the nature of the country they inhabited. In a mountainous country it would be less; in a plain country more. In Persia it is usually reckoned at about 4 miles, and in the flat country of 'Irāq-'Arabī, to which the author of the Chach Nāma no doubt belonged, it would most likely be about the same. But the most usual method of reckoning distances in olden times was by the day's journey—as vague and various a standard as the farsakh—but in a plain country, where no exceptional obstacles to progress were met with, commonly taken at about 20 miles. Ibnu Hawqil says (Elliot, I. 30, where, however, *Tiz* is clearly a mistake for

[63] The writers quoted speak of the mouth of the "Mihrān," but they need not be held to refer to the main river, but only to that branch of it on which Dēbal was situated. At that time, according to the Ashkālu'l-Belād map, Dēbal was not on the main stream, though how far from it it is impossible to conjecture, the cartographer having had no notion of scale.

Nīrūn) Nīrūn was 4 days' from Debal, meaning, of course, by the direct route ordinarily followed by travellers, and by that route Kakar Bukēra is a little more than 80 miles from Ḫaydarābād. By the route, however, which the Arab force took the distance, as we shall see hereafter, would be much more, and would certainly not be under but rather above 100 miles. The march occupied, we are told, 6 days, that is slightly more than 16 miles a day, a very fair rate of progress for a force obliged to keep as near the river as possible and to regulate its daily advance by that of the convoy under its protection. We thus have statements of distance by the different routes and by the different observers which go to support the proposed identification.

For all these reasons then, I am led to think that Kakar Bukēra is the site of ancient Dēwal, and that all the evidence is against the identifications of the famous Delta port with Karāchī, Lāhorī Bandar, or Ṭhaṭa, each of which has had its confident supporters.[64]

[64] Captain Burton was positive as to Ṭhaṭa. "We are certain" (he says) "that the modern Tatta occupies the ground of the ancient Dēwal, as the Arabs and Persians know it by no other name—Shal-i-Dibali still being used to mean a shawl of Tatta manufactory" (Sindh, II. n. 2). That Thata was called Dēwal by Arab traders is certain. Sir A. Burnes says ("Cabul," p. 17): "When last I was in Bombay the native agent at Muscat in Arabia wrote as a matter of news that the Iman was about to attack Zanguebar and had sent to Dēwal to hire soldiers; he had applied to Sinde for mercenaries." Another illustration of the linking of the names of Ṭhaṭa and Dēwal is found in a manuscript report of Mr. Crow, British commercial agent at Ṭhaṭa in the last year or two of last century. He speaks of "the ruins of a city said to be ancient *Thata*, or *Dewal Sindi*, on the eastern (northern) bank of this creek (the Ghāra: he refers to the ruins of Bhambhor) about 40 miles from its mouth. There is the ruin of another, it is said, still more ancient, *Thata*, or *Dewal Sindi*, in the heart of the Delta." (This may refer to the Bukēra site, but there are many old sites in the Delta.) The Portuguese, who became acquainted with the Delta country in the sixteenth century, called Lāhorī Bandar *Diul*, and Sindh *Diulcinde*, and at a later period the English did the same. Faria y Souza, in his work on Asia, speaks of "the city *Diul* seated on the westernmost mouth of Indus." (Stevens' Translation, II. 514.) The fact is that the fame of ancient Dēwal, in consequence of its commercial importance, and also, perhaps, from the quasi-sacred character attaching to the place, caused its name to survive long after the port had been abandoned and its buildings had fallen to ruin. The foreign traders transferred its name to its successor as a Delta port, called by Sindhīs "Lāhorī," and even to all the Western Delta, and its chief town, Ṭhaṭa, when that came into existence. But there is no evidence to show that by the natives of Sindh Ṭhaṭa was ever called Dēwal, though it is true that one native writer has made the careless statement that "Dēwal is Thata." The Ṭhaṭa people themselves do not hold that view, for a Seyyid of the place, who had given some attention to the question, told me that he had taken much trouble to discover where Dēwal had been situated, and had never been able to solve the difficulty.

Sir Henry Elliot would at once have abandoned the Karāchī identification if he had been aware that that place is, by the shortest route, 110 miles from the actual site of Nīrūm, while he held that the equivalent of 25 farsakhs could not at the utmost be more than 75 miles. As to Lāhorī Bandar it need only be said that its situation among a number of tidal channels, isolating it from the country inland, would render it most unsuitable for a substantially constructed town. Its river distance, too, from the sea is only sixteen miles; while, according to Masūdī, Dēbal was at least twice that distance from the sea. And if Lāhorī Bandar is Dēwal, how are we to explain the fact of the disappearance of its former celebrated name and its replacement by one utterly insignificant in comparison? The Thata site is still more out of the question. It is surprising that its distance from the sea, and the difficulty of navigation by keeled ships of such a river as the Indus have been overlooked by those who are "certain" that it was once a famous port for sea-going vessels! It is at the very least twice too far inland to have ever served such a purpose.

Dēwal, besides being a commercial port, was also a settlement of pirates, belonging to a tribe who were called Nagāmara.[66] It was the capture and the plundering by these sea-rovers of certain subjects of the Khalīfa, and the refusal of redress by Prince Dāhir, then on the throne at Alor, that led to the Arab invasion of Sindh; or perhaps it would be more in accordance with truth to say that it precipitated that event. For many years previous to the affair of the pirates the Arab commanders on the eastern frontier of Mekrān had been engaged in entirely unprovoked and wanton raids into western Sindh from Qayqānān (the modern Gandāva) down to Sēwan; and on any fair consideration of matters in dispute between the two powers Prince Dāhir had far more cause of complaint than the Khalīfa. The real fact was that the fertile Indus Valley, and the wealth to be gained there by a victorious army, offered an irresistible temptation to the needy Arabs, and invasion could be only a question of time and opportunity. The first attempts at reprisal for the piratical outrage issued in disaster. Two successive attacks on Dēwal were completely defeated, with the loss of the commander of each expedi-

[66] Sir H. Elliot calls them Tangāmara, saying at the same time that there is a difficulty about his first letter. I think the name in the text is the correct one, though I am not sure that I have not heard them called in Sindh *Nigāmara*.

tion. The shame of these reverses at the hands of infidels and grief at the death of Budhayl, a favourite who led the second expedition, preyed upon the mind of Hajjāj, the Governor of 'Irāq, who held the chief control of the Khalīfa's eastern dependencies; and when after a long delay a considerable force was sent to conquer Sindh, he gave the commander orders not to spare the people of Dēwal. The three days' slaughter carried out in too faithful compliance with this injunction, the destruction of the temple which had given name to the place, and the exhaustive pillaging which was added to the other horrors of the capture, must have left Dēwal a mere wreck. Yet it survived, and in time apparently recovered a considerable degree of prosperity. The capture by the Arabs occurred most probably in 710 A.D. (the exact date is uncertain). Some time in the last quarter of the twelfth century, nearly 500 years later, Sulṭān Jalālu'd-Dīn Khwārasmī invaded Sindh, passed into the Delta country, took Dēwal and the surrounding territory, and "acquired much wealth."[66] A large proportion of this "wealth" must have been the result of plundering Dēwal, as outside of the few towns or larger villages which it contained, the Delta country could have offered little to excite the greed of the raider. Again, in the year 1223 A.D. the same prince, flying before the victorious Chingīz Khān, took refuge in the Delta, and for a time rested in Dēwal.[67] This is one of the latest, if not quite the latest, notices of Dēwal as still existing and inhabited.[68] Rather more than a century later, in 1333 or 1334, when Ibnu Baṭuṭa was in the Delta, Dēwal was no more: at least no mention of it occurs in the traveller's narrative, and its place as a port had been taken by *Lāharī* (Lāharī Bandar) twenty miles farther down the Baghār Channel. The probability is that Dēwal was abandoned in con-

[66] See the "Ṭabakāt-i-Nāṣirī" in Major Raverty's translation, vol. i. p. 452. Among works dealing with any considerable portion of eastern history, this of Major Raverty's is quite monumental in respect of its painstaking accuracy and its instructive and exhaustive comment. He justly describes the work, "text and notes together," as a "very thesaurus of most varied and often recondite historical material for the period of which it treats." What a pity that its value should be grievously impaired by the want of an index!

[67] Ibid. n. pp. 294–5.

[68] It is possible that the Dēwal of Jalālu'd-Dīn's day was not the original Dēwal, but some other town to which the famous name had been transferred. It is curious that El Birūni, writing in the first half of the eleventh century, does not name Dēwal, but speaks of *Lohārānī* as apparently the Delta port of that time.

sequence of the Baghār's increasing shoaling preventing the access of sea-going vessels to the port.[69]

Dēwal having been captured and secured as a base for further operations, the invading force moved northward into the interior, *Nīrūn* being the next point aimed at. The siege-train, consisting of catapults, some of which were of large size, was sent up country in boats by a branch of the Indus called *Sind Sāgar*. This Sanscrit name, of which *Sind Daryā*, or "Sind Sea," is the modern Persianized equivalent, is mentioned by El Birūnī in connection with the Indus. Speaking of the course of that river in Sindh he describes it as dividing at Manṣūra, and then "flowing into the ocean at two places near the city Lohārānī, and more eastward in the province of Ka<u>chch</u>ha at a place called *Sindhu-Sāgara, i.e.* the Sindh Sea." On the other hand Reshīdu'd-Dīn, whose work the Jāmi'ut-Tawārī<u>kh</u>, completed in 1310 A.D., "is really and confessedly" a Persian version of El Birūnī's "India" (Elliot, I. 42), gives El Birūnī's description in this form: "At this place (Manṣūra) the river divides into two streams; one empties itself into the sea in the neighbourhood of the city of Lūhārānī, and the other branches off to the east to the borders of Kach, *and is known by the name of Sind-Sāgar, i.e. "Sea of Sind"* (Ibid. p. 49). The name would certainly be more appropriate to a river, and one of considerable size, than to a "*place*"; and when we find in the Chach Nāma that in the eighth century there was a branch of the Indus actually so called, it is permissible to suspect some corruption in the existing texts of Birūnī, and to conjecture that the one used by Reshīdu'd-Dīn contained the correct reading. But if the Sindhu-Sāgara was an eastward flowing branch, reaching the sea by the borders of Ka<u>chch</u>ha, that is, through the Korī Creek, the reported proceeding of the Arab commander in sending his siege-train by such a circuitous route, and one that would carry it in an

[69] Of the period of the foundation of Dēwal nothing is known. The place seems to have been in existence as early as the commencement of the Rae dynasty, which Elliot puts about 495 A.D. ("History" I. 407 and 138). It was known to Chinese navigators in the seventh century. The late Sir H. Yule in "Cathay and the Way Thither" (I. lxxviii.), says: "Chinese annals of the Thang dynasty, of the seventh and eighth centuries, describe the course followed by their junks in voyaging to the Euphrates from Kwangcheu (Canton)." After describing the course as rounding Ceylon and following the coast northward till they reached Tiyu (or Diu), he proceeds: "Ten days' further voyage carried them past five small kingdoms to another Tiyu, near the great Milan or Sintu." This, of course, was Dēwal on the Mihrān or Indus.

unexplored and hostile country, far from the possibility of protection by the rest of the army, eventually landing it (if, by a miracle, it escaped capture or destruction) at a great distance from Nirūn, becomes totally inexplicable and incredible. And not less inexplicable is the presumption involved that no other Delta stream besides this farthest eastern one was then navigable for any distance by boats. The only possible solution of the difficulty seems to lie in the supposition that there were *two* Sindh-Sāgaras, and in favour of such a supposition there is some ground more solid than a plausible conjecture. Arrian tells us that both the main Delta branches in Alexander's time were "large rivers and both preserved the name *Indus* down to the sea." If this is correct, then the *indigenous* name of each was certainly *Sindhu,* and the old Sanscrit name, preserved by El Birūnī, of *Sindhu-Sāgara* would equally apply to both, since it is impossible to believe that a name implying great breadth and volume would attach more to the eastern than to the western branch, which latter indeed had perhaps the greater claim to it (see above, p. 29, *n.* 44). Now we have seen (above, pp. 9, 10) that there is strong evidence to support the belief that the present Ghāro is part of the channel—the great western branch—by which Alexander, and after him Nearchus, sailed down to the sea, and it is beyond question the channel which Ptolemy calls *Sagapa*. That Sagapa may very likely be a corruption of Sāgara will be accepted without argument by the most critical, and there can be no difficulty in believing that the correct and complete name was Sindhu-Sāgara.[70] And some further and curious support of the theory that the present Ghāro is the remnant of the western Sindhu-Sāgara is found in a statement occuring incidentally in the Chach Nāma. There it is said that the Arab commander "ordered the catapults to be embarked on boats and forwarded towards the fort of Nīrūn. *They brought the boats into the river* called Sind Sāgar."[71] This statement makes it

[70] It will, perhaps, be asked why, if Sāgara was the real name of the eastern branch '*down to the sea,*' does Ptolemy call the mouth of that branch Lonibare and not Sagara? The explanation probably is that the eastern Sindhu-Sāgara was considered to end either where it reached the Ran of Kachchha, or at its junction with the Loni, which was most likely a few miles north-east of Lakhpat. From this point the channel down to the sea may have been called the Loni Estuary (Lonibare). During his hurried voyage to the sea by the eastern channel Alexander may not have learnt this fact, or it may have escaped his historians.

[71] "Kishtī dar āb kih ānrā Sind Sāgar goyand mī burdand." This is incorrectly rendered in Elliot's "History" (I. 157) "The boats *went up* the stream which they call Sind Sāgar."

clear that Dēwal was not on the Sindhu-Sāgara, for if it had been so situated the boats would have been in that stream already.[72] Now in seeking for the site of Dēwal it is evident, as I trust I have proved, that our field of choice is limited to the lands on the Ghāro and Baghār. On the bank of one or other of these two channels the town must have stood, and it seems certain that the one on which it did *not* stand was the Sindhu-Sāgara, because no other Delta channel would have been equally convenient for a flotilla proceeding to the neighbourhood of Nīrūn, and probably by no other channel could it have gone into the interior under effective protection from the army proceeding by land. Thus if it be conceded that Dēwal was on the Baghār, it becomes an almost unavoidable conclusion that the Ghāro channel is the remnant of the ancient Sindhu-Sāgara.[73]

But assuming this conclusion to be established, there remains the interesting question whether the channel of the Sindhu-Sāgara was still complete at the time of the Arab invasion, and, though not a permanent stream, yet in activity during the flood-season ; or whether its continuity had already been broken by the turning of the stream into a southerly course as described in the first section (pp. 6. 7). Here we have no positive evidence to guide us. In support of the view that the channel was then not continuous, or at least contained little

[72] The siege-train had been brought from 'Irāq to Dēwal by sea, but for the navigation of the Indus higher up than Dēwal the sea-going vessels would have been totally unsuited : these must have been left at Dēwal and ordinary river-craft employed in the further operations.

[73] Against this conclusion it may be urged that Ptolemy's names for the river mouths cannot be quoted in decisive support of it. For if it is *most probable* that Sagapa ought to be corrected to Sagara, it is *absolutely certain* that Sinthon (the name of the second mouth from the west) is the Greek form of Sindhu,* and this may be held fairly to raise the presumption that the Sinthon, and not the Sagapa, was the mouth of the Sindhu-Sāgara which would thus be identical with the Baghār and its prolongations. If this were accepted it would follow, on the reasoning in the text, that Dēwal was on the Ghāro, and, as an equally necessary conclusion, that that channel was in full activity and navigable for several miles by sea-going vessels in the beginning of the eighth century ; that in short nothing had changed during the 1000 years which had elapsed since Alexander's expedition, the "westing" of the river farther inland having been suspended for ten centuries. Rather than accept such conclusions, it seems to me preferable to suppose that when the second mouth became the principal embouchure the name Sindhu was transferred to it while the remaining portion of the name was retained for the old mouth.

* If there were a doubt on this point it would be removed by the fact that in another section of his Geography (Lib. vii. I. § 28) Ptolemy calls this same mouth *Indos*.

or no water, it may be said that there is no mention in the histories of the invaders having crossed any Delta channel on their way to Dēwal. But the narrative might have been equally silent on the subject though there had been a stream to cross, since, if such was the case, the crossing was not opposed. For the historians the real starting point of the campaign was the siege of Dēwal, and though there is a casual reference to the "capture of Armāil" (near Las Bēla), nothing of any interest is recorded during the long march from Shīrāz, where the army assembled, to the great town in the Indus Delta. On the other hand, if the old Sindhu-Sāgara was then still flowing and unfordable the Sindhians would hardly have neglected the precaution of removing all boats from the stream, and would probably have offered some armed opposition to the passage. In this case there would have been some delay which, especially when connected with the first collision, however slight, with the Sindhians, would certainly have been noticed. To this consideration must be added the improbability of a town of the size and substantial character of Dēwal being built in a position where it would be separated from the mainland by a stream such as the Sindhu-Sāgara must have been when in full activity. If that stream was flowing and nagivable when Dēwal was founded, it is difficult to see why a site was not chosen on its bank rather than on that of the Baghār, where stone for the more solid buildings would have to be carried ten miles farther than would be necessary if the place were founded on the Sindhu-Sāgara. On the whole then, the weight of probability seems to be against the supposition that the old channel of the Sindhu-Sāgara was still continuous in the eighth century; and if it was not so we must take that name, as used in the Chach Nāma, to apply to the present *Kalrī*, a little north of Ṭhaṭa, and to a considerable stretch of the river beyond it—as far northward probably as the twenty-fifth parallel—in fact to about the latitude of the great bifurcation of Alexander's time. And the channel through which the boats were "brought into the Sindhu-Sāgara" must have been that now known as the *K͟hānāh*—the later course of the Sindhu-Sāgara when it changed from westward to southward—which joined the Baghār close to my site of Dēwal.

The existence of a western as well as an eastern Sindhu-Sāgara being now established, the arrangements for the conveyance of the siege-train become intelligible. The flotilla went up the western

Sindhu-Sāgara under the protection of the army which marched along the right bank.[74] The course of the Indus, it will be borne in mind, was then, as for centuries afterwards, very far to the east of the present one, and after the Sindhu-Sāgara had been reached the direction of the march would be for some distance due east and then north till some point probably south-east of Nīrūn was gained when, after disembarking the siege-train, the army would march on that fort. The total length of this somewhat circuitous route from Dēwal to Nīrūn would be at least one hundred miles, or, as stated in the Chach Nāma, twenty-five "farsakhs," a fact which suffices to show that the site of Dēwal cannot have been much, if at all, to the west of the point I assign to it; for instance, not at or near Lāhorī Bandar (as General Cunningham thinks it was) from which place the march would have been at least 120 miles.

Nīrūn stood, as already stated, on the ground now occupied by Ḫaydarābād fort. "Here" (says the Chach Nāma) "there is a grassy tract called *Balahār* in the district of *Barūī* (or *Barrī*), and as yet the water of the river Mihrān had not come there, and the army suffered severely from thirst." Balahār and Barūī are names that, so far as I know, have long since vanished from the locality, and are not to be recognised in any of those now existing. The reference to the water of the Mihrān can only be understood as indicating that a canal or canals brought water from the Indus to the country around Nīrūn during the time of the inundation (May to September), but were dry during the rest of the year. The Indus, if it then flowed in the old abandoned channel still to be seen to the east of Ḫaydarābād, was some sixteen miles distant from Nīrūn, and may have been much farther. Nīrūn was evidently a place of little importance and no particular strength. Though its gates were at first closed against the Arabs, it was soon surrendered without any fighting. Such value as it possessed seems to have consisted in its situation on the main road from the capital Alor, by the ancient city of Brahmanābād, and afterwards by Manṣūra, to the port of Dēwal. Idrīsī, who compiled his Geography in the twelfth century, says: "Nīrūn is half way between

[74] If the old channel was then still in activity the army must have re-crossed it soon after leaving Dēwal, but of this there is no mention. The Sindhian Prince and the bulk of his forces remained in the country east of the Indus throughout the campaign; and as it was the Arab commander's object to secure his rear by gaining possession of Nīrūn and Siwastān before striking the decisive blow at the main Sindhian army, it was for the present essential to keep to the right bank of the Indus.

Debal and Manṣūra, and people going from one town to the other *here cross the river*" (Elliot, I. 78)—a remark which, being unexplained in Elliot's History, would lead its readers to suppose that the Indus ran close to Nīrūn. Idrīsī, however, was simply copying Ibnu Hawqil, but going wrong in names. The latter says correctly: "*Manjābarī* is to the west of the Mihrān, and *there* any one who proceeds from Dēbal to Manṣūra will have to pass the river, the latter place being opposite to Manjābarī" (Elliot, I. 37). Another remark of Idrīsī, and similarly misleading, is left without comment by Elliot's editor. He says, describing the course of the Indus below Mansūra: "The Mihrān passes on *to* Nīrūn" (Ibid. p. 78), when, in fact, it was never, down to the middle of the eighteenth century, within 15 or 16 miles of the site of Nīrūn. The *Phulēlī*, an inundation channel, now running under the eastern flank of the ridge on which Ḫaydarābād fort stands, is not, contrary to General Cunningham ("An. Geog. of India," p. 279), to be thought of as existing in the eighth century, because it has its head in the present course of the Indus, some 12 miles north of Ḫaydarābād, and that course, as already mentioned, was taken by the river so late as last century. For the statement by General Cunningham, that there was a lake near Nīrūn "of sufficient size to receive the fleet of Muhammed Kāsim" (Ibid. p. 280), there is no authority in the Chach Nāma, which speaks only of a *pool* of water (ābgīr) in the vicinity of the fort. If there was a *lake* there, the account of the army's suffering severely from thirst until rain fell and filled, as we are told, "all the pools and reservoirs in the lands around the town," must evidently be a mere fiction.

The Campaign of Sīwastān.

Though the Sīwastān campaign lies, properly speaking, outside the scope of this memoir, some notice of it seems desirable, with a view both to obtain a further idea of the course of the Indus at that time, and also to complete the account of the military operations in the country west of the river as detailed in the Chach Nāma.

After gaining possession of Nīrūn the army proceeded against Sīwastān (Sēwaṉ), and "advanced by stages till it reached a place called *Moj*, distant 30 farsakhs from Nīrūn." Thus some place (Moj cannot be identified) which, as the narrative implies, was not so far, as Sīwastān is said to be about 120 miles from Nīrūn, while we know that the entire distance between Ḩaydarābād and Sēwan̲ is little more than 80 miles. This excessive discrepancy between positive fact and the statement of the Chach Nāma, while it seems to discredit that chronicle, is perhaps in reality a striking proof of its general trustworthiness. The explanation I take to be that the army marched by the hill route, though not a hint is given of this having been the case, unless such is to be found in the fact that the Arab commander took with him the native governor of Nīrūn as guide, which would hardly have been necessary for so simple a march as the direct one from Nīrūn to Sīwastān. The distance by the hill-route is 110 miles, and to Moj, which seems to have been close to Sīwastān, would be something less. It may be assumed that by 30 farsakhs we are to understand 7 or 8 marches. The reason of this indirect and much longer route having been selected is apparent enough on strategical grounds. The effective fighting forces of Sindh were gathered in and about Brahmanābād; that is to say, at the apex of a triangle of which the line Nīrūn-Sīwastān was the base. Had the Arab commander marched along this line both his right flank and rear would have been exposed to attack by the Sindhian prince, who still commanded all the resources of the country and could have crossed the river at any point he pleased; while in front of the Arabs, and at no great distance, were the as yet intact forces of western Sindh. These last, indeed, were soon to prove themselves anything but formidable, but in recent years, as we learn from the Chach Nāma, they had inflicted a crushing defeat on an Arab raiding force which had entered Sindh by one of the north-western passes, and they could not be left out of account as a factor of no importance in such a combination as was quite feasible if the Sindhian Prince chose to give it effect. On the other hand, the hill-route would not only place double the distance between the Arabs and the Eastern Sindhians, but would also guarantee to the former complete protection to their flanks by hill-ranges, and, Nīrūn being held, immunity from attack on their rear. The hill country would present no difficulties to the light marching Arab force, and as it never can have supported more than a very scanty population, no opposition would be met with from the hill-people.[75]

[75] At certain times of the year there would be difficulty about water for a force consisting of some thousands, but, as we shall presently see, the march took place at a time of the year when rain may have fallen and water may have been abundant in

On reaching Sīwastān, the Arab commander, says the narrative, "encamped before the Rēgistān gate, because there was no other position suitable for conducting warlike operations, and the floods of the rainy season (varshākāla) were at their height and were flowing through the stream *Sindhu Aral* on the northern side of the fortress."[76] Sīwastān is described in the Chach Nāma as situated "*to the west of the Mihrān*," but it is not said that the place was on, or near, the river. The Indus, indeed, is never once mentioned during the Sīwastān campaign, and it is probable that at this time it was flowing perhaps ten miles, perhaps twenty-five miles, to the east of its present course near Sēwan̲, for at both those distances abandoned and very ancient river channels are to be seen. In this case the Aral must have had a course of several miles to the south-east of Sēwan̲, all trace of which has since been obliterated by the westward movement of the Indus. The antiquity of the Aral is thus established, and with it that of the western Nārā also, the Aral being, in fact, the Nārā after the reappearance of the latter from the Manchur lake. The western Nārā, indeed, must be one of the most ancient branch streams of the Indus, for Sēwan̲ must have been for ages dependent on it for its water-supply. And Sēwan̲ is not only the oldest of inhabited towns in Sindh, but is probably older than—or at least as old as—any of those whose sites are now only faintly traced in mounds of brick-dust and broken pottery, and whose names have perished. Of the places in Sindh mentioned by Alexander's historians, the only one that can be identified with the remotest degree of approximation to probability is Sēwan̲, which is almost certainly the *Sindomana* (perhaps for *Saindhavān*) of the Greeks. This long endurance it owes to its position originally far to the west

the Kohistān. In the cold season of 1840–41 a wing of a British Dragoon Regiment marched by this route from Sēwan̲ to Karāchī.

[76] The text is here in some confusion, especially in regard to the name of the stream. Sir H. Elliot's copy read: "Jūī Sindh wa rāwal," and the India Office Library copy (a far better one) "jūī Sind dar awal." There can be no doubt, however, as to the stream that is intended. It is the *Aral* which flows round Sēwan on the north and east, and ارل has been turned into راول, and در اول. Most probably the name was Sindhu-Aral (سندھ أرل) which may have at first been written سندوارل. The Rēgistān is a sandy tract extending southward from Sēwan̲ to the so-called *Lakī* range. The "floods of the rainy season" may mean simply the usual inundation floods, the expression not necessarily implying that rain had fallen. The time, however, was almost certainly July or August when there is usually a few days' rain in Sindh.

of the Indus, and beyond the range of that destructive river's encroachment; and in modern times, when at length the Indus touched its very walls, to its foundation on the low rocky ridge underlying the sandy tract between the Aral and the Lakī Hills; to which must be added the long constancy of the western Nārā.[77]

The resistance of Sīwastān, paralysed by internal dissensions and disaffection, lasted little more than a week. The governor then "crossed the stream (the Aral) near the northern gate by night and fled to Būdhīya." The district so named is frequently mentioned in the Chach Nāma, and by the Arab geographers. It lay to the west of the Indus, and its southern limit seems to have been about forty miles north of Sēwan̲, since it is said to have been five days from Manṣūra.[78] The Chach Nāma, describing the territorial subdivisions of Sindh in the time of Rāe Sīharas (about the middle of the sixth century A.D.) says that one of these included "the town of Sīwastān (and most probably some territory around it) together with *Būdhīya, Jangāl*[79] and the hill-country of *Dūnjhān* as far as the borders of Makrān." Again in the seventh century, when the Brahman Chach was on the throne, that prince is said to have crossed to the west bank of the Indus in Upper Sindh into Būdhīya and, after taking its chief town, *Kākārāj*, he proceeded to Sīwastān, where the governor, like him of Kākārāj, had declared himself independent, and had to be reduced to obedience. It is thus plain that Būdhīya was the name of a district conterminous with that of Sīwastān on the north. From the narrative of the further course of

[77] In the maps (so-called) of Istakhri and Ibnu Hawqil, which are not to be regarded as quite independent productions, Sīwastān (or Sadūsān) appears actually on the bank of the Indus, and in his text Ibnu Hawqil uses language indicating that such was the case. These geographers describe the country as it was about 250 years after the Arab conquest, when the river had no doubt "wested" a great deal. If they are right, then the Indus at the time of the Arab conquest cannot have been more than 8 to 10 miles east of Sēwan̲.

[78] It would thus nearly coincide with the southern boundary of the Kakar Pargana, and of the Shikārpur Division west of the Indus, though there is some reason for thinking a part of it may have extended farther south and touched the Manchur lake. Ibnu Hawqil calls the distance from Manṣūra 15 days, but this is clearly an error, as it would place Būddhīya quite outside modern Sindh and in the Derājāt, while it is evident from the Chach Nāma, and from Istakhri, that it was not very far from Sēwan̲. The Arab geographers call it *Buda*.

[79] This may perhaps be identified with Jhāngār, a very ancient township, 13 miles west of Sēwan̲ and close to the northern border of the hill country.

the Sīwastān campaign, it may perhaps be gathered that Būdhīya included the lands lying between the western Nārā and the mountain ranges west of Sēwaṉ. It is stated that when Bachra, the governor of Sīwastān, escaped from that fortress, he fled to the governor of Būdhīya, whose "stronghold was *Sīsam* on the shore of a "*Kumbh.*" This last word may mean a "lake" such as the Manchur, or a piece of water that would properly be called a "pond." It is mentioned again in connection with another place which it is perhaps possible to identify. When the Arab commander had made himself master of the fortress of Sīwastān he marched in pursuit of Bachra, and "encamped at a place called *Nidhān* on the shore of a (or the) Kumbh." In Sir H. Elliot's copy of the Chach Nāma this place appears as *Nilhān.* In the Arabic character the difference between the two names as written is very slight, and the transposition of a dot would convert the initial *nūn* in each into *ba,* when we should have *Bidhān* and *Bilhān,* and it is at once seen how easily copyists may have written either instead of *Bilhaṉ.* This last name belongs to a village and township on the Manchur lake, seven miles west of Sēwaṉ. Most of the township-names round the Manchur lake are probably very ancient, but one at all events, being Muhammedan, cannot have been in existence at this time. This is Shāh-Ḫasan, belonging to a township at the western end of the lake beyond the Nārā river, which must have supplanted some earlier Hindū name, and I would suggest that the latter may have been *Sīsam.* That in the course of many centuries, and under predominant Muhammedan influences, such a name has lapsed from all memory and tradition, is only what might be expected. At all events the suggested identifications of Nilhān, or Nidhān, and Sīsam fit in well with all the circumstances of the Sīwastān campaign as these are to be gathered from the Chach Nāma, and I am unable to point to any others of which as much can be said. A stronghold of the Būdhīya district being near at hand, and the late governor of Sīwastān,[80] as well as the governor of Būdhīya, being there, its capture would naturally suggest itself to the Arab commander as essential to the security of Sīwastān and the territory belonging to it. In advancing on Sīsam he would halt at Bilhaṉ, about half-way from Sīwastān to the fortress at the west end of the Manchur lake, and in a

[80] A person of importance, being a cousin of Dāhir, prince of Sindh.

second march he would cross the western Nārā and reach his point.[81] On the supposition that Nidhān and Sīsam have here been correctly identified, it follows that the Nārā formed the boundary between Sīwastān and Būdhīya on the west.

While the Arabs were encamped at Nidhān the Jats of Sīsam projected a night attack on them. This failed in consequence of the Jats neglecting to keep together, and to their going astray in the darkness. Hereupon the Chief of Būdhīya made his submission though his people continued to resist till, after two days' fighting, Sīsam was taken. On this occasion Bachra and several other chiefs "lost their lives (says the narrative) through their opposition, and the remainder fled to the more northern part of Būdhīya. Some went to the fort of *Bhatlor* between *Sāloj* and Qandhābīl,[82] and thence sent a request for a letter of protection because they were at enmity with Dāhir on account of his having killed some of their number. For this reason they abandoned allegiance to him, and sending messengers (to M. Qāsim) to mediate, they imposed on themselves a tribute of 1000 silver dirams, and also sent hostages to Sīwastān." With the capture of Sīsam the short and successful campaign of Sīwastān came to an end. At this place the Arab commander received a letter from Ḫajjāj, the governor of 'Irāq, directing him to return to Nīrūn and make preparations for crossing the Mihrān, which he at once did, but by what route is not said.

The Sīwastān campaign is interesting, if for nothing else yet for the fact that we now begin to perceive, what comes out still more plainly in the next and most important scenes of the invasion, that the Arabs were not wholly dependent for their success on the ability

[81] At the present day it would be impossible to move troops in this part of the country in July or August, when, as has been shown, the Sīwastān campaign took place, owing to the swelling of the lake and the overflowing of the Nārā during the inundation; but in the eighth century, the Indus being much farther to the east throughout Sindh than it is now, the western districts were no doubt much drier than at present when the floods from the river sometimes put the whole of ancient Sīwastān and Būdhīya under water.

[82] I am unable to suggest any identification of Bhaṭlor, or Sāloj. Qandhābīl (probably the now ruined Gandāva) was the chief town of *Qayqānān*, a district which included the modern Kachhī and perhaps the country east of it as far as the Indus. Būdhīya seems to have extended on the north up to Qayqānān. This last district is mentioned by Hiuen Tsang, who calls it *Ki-ka-na*, and says it was reported to be celebrated for its horses, which indeed has been a fact in all ages. The Khalifas themselves, with the fine Arabian breeds at their disposal, were glad to replenish their stables from Qayqānān.

of their young leader[83] and their own valour. It was their fortune to undertake the conquest of Sindh at a time when the struggle between Buddhism and Brahmanism was still in progress, when a weak prince was on the throne, and disaffection and treason were rife. We find frequent mention of *Samanīs* in the Chach Nāma. This was the form which the Arabs gave to the appellative *Shramana*, by which the class of Buddhist ascetics was known, but they appear to have applied it to Buddhists holding positions of authority as well as to those who were actually monks or devotees. The governor of Nīrūn was a Samanī, and he showed alacrity in surrendering to the Arabs. At Moj,[84] where M. Qāsīm halted before beginning the siege of Sīwastān, the leading man was a Samanī. He received the Arabs with cordiality, and with his brother Samanīs exhorted the governor of Sīwastān to make his submission. "We are Nāsiks" (they wrote to him); "our religion is one of peace and our profession is averse from violence. You dwell in a lofty citadel, but we have to fear loss of life and property from the Arabs." When the governor resolved to fight they remonstrated, saying: "You cannot contend with the Arab force: life and property must not be brought to destruction through your obstinacy." And when this proved unavailing they resorted to open treason, writing to Muhammed Qāsim: "The population which consists of cultivators, artisans, traders, and the lowest sort are ill-disposed to Bachra, and are not bound to him. He has no forces to oppose to you, and cannot give you battle." Thus encouraged, the Arab leader prosecuted the siege with vigour and soon gained possession of Sīwastān. The governor of Būdhīya was a Samanī. He did his utmost to dissuade his people from resistance, and, failing in his unpatriotic object, went over to M. Qāsim and actually aided him in plundering the country, capturing Sīsam, and slaying or dispersing the chiefs of Būdhīya. Among these chiefs themselves there was dissatisfaction owing to an act of severity on the part of Prince Dāhir, and though they did make one stand for their country that effort sufficed to exhaust their courage and loyalty, and they followed the general example of their order in speedily submitting to the invader.

[83] He was only 17 years of age when appointed by his uncle Ḥajjāj to the command of the Sindh Expedition, and he cannot have been more than 21 or 22 when he was tortured and executed, in pursuance of a blood-feud, by Ḥajjāj's successor in 'Irāq.

[84] Moj may have been a kind of suburb of Sīwastān where there was a Buddhist settlement or a monastery.

In recording all this, the chronicler fails not to give the story that dash of colouring which is essential if Muslim taste is to be satisfied. The advent of Islām is found to have been long predicted in the country. At Dēwal, M. Qāṣim had this encouraging assurance from two different authorities of that place. The Chief of Būdhīya, endeavouring to dishearten his people who desired to fight, informs them that the monks have found in their astrological books that "this territory is to be conquered by the army of Islām." After his defection he repeats the same thing to M. Qāsim, tells him that in the failure of the attempted night-attack "a miracle has been manifested," that it is certain that the conquest of Sindh has been divinely decreed, and concludes: "As for me I make my submission, and will give you my advice and be your guide in the conquering and overthrowing of your enemies." Such was the state of things as seen in the light of Muhammedan imagination. But the consultation of seers and astrologers in order to ascertain what were the divine decrees, must have been quite superfluous for people endowed with ordinary powers of observation, who could see those decrees written plainly in a kingdom divided against itself by religious antagonism, in the feebleness and misgovernment of its prince and the universal disloyalty of the ruling class.

All Western Sindh, with perhaps the exception of Qayqānān, had now abandoned its allegiance to its native prince and accepted the rule of the Khalīfa. Some time later, indeed, there was an insignificant rising against the Arab garrison in the town of Sīwastān, one Chandarām Hāla heading it, but it was quickly suppressed; and so much confidence had the Arab commander in the disaffection towards the late ruler now prevalent in Western Sindh, that he actually drew 4000 men from the Sīwastān country to recruit his army which was about to cross the Indus and enter on the final struggle with Prince Dāhir.[85] A further proof of this disaffection, combined perhaps with

[85] The men levied in Sīwastān were *Jats*—a fact not mentioned by the Chach Nāma on this occasion, but stated by Bilādhurī. Later, however, we read in the Chach Nāma of the "western Jats" who were serving with the Arabs, an illustration of the agreement yet independence of the two narratives. By a ludicrous blunder these western Jats become in Elliot's translation (Hist. I. 167) the "Jats of *Ghaznī*" !! the text having, through a misplacement of dots, غزني for غربي. For convenience sake the invading force is throughout this memoir called the "Arab" force, but it was really, in respect of the nationalities of its constituent bodies, a very composite army. The total strength of the invaders when they started from Shirāz appears to

the awe inspired by the Arabs, is supplied by the fact that M. Qāsim could detach so small a body as 600 horsemen from the army, then in Lower Central Sindh, to such a distance as Bakhar (*Baghrūr*) in order to observe Alor (by which the river was then running) and hinder Prince Dāhir's son from making any diversion against the communications of the invaders.

From Nīrūn the Arabs moved against a fortified place called in the Chach Nāma *Ashbhār,* and by Bilādhuri سهار, all pointing being omitted. This place cannot be identified, but it seems to have been situated not far from Nīrūn, or from the Indus, as the next move was to the bank of the river which seems to have been accomplished in one march. Ashbhār surrendered after a week's siege, and no further resistance was offered by any place to the west of the Indus. It appears that western Sindh had been completely subdued in the space of just one year.[86]

It is difficult to conjecture at what spot the Arabs crossed the Indus. The Chach Nāma describes it as a place opposite the fort of *Jaham,* which appears to have been the principal stronghold of the district called *Bet,* on the east side of the river, which I am unable to identity. Bilādhurī says the crossing took place at a point adjoining the country of Rāsal, chief of *Qassa* in Hind. Qaṣṣa (قصه) is the nearest Arabic approach to Kachchh, just as Ṣaṣṣa (صصه) is to Chach, the letter *cha* being unknown in Arabic and unpronounceable by Arabs. We must not suppose, however, that the place of crossing was anywhere near the territory of modern Kachchh. In ancient times that province extended far to the north of its present limits—

have been 12,000 men, of whom 6,000 were Syrians—by special request of Hajjāj, picked men and of good families (Hajjaj's experience of 'Irāq Arabs had led him to distrust and detest them, while he had good reason to place full confidence in Syrian troops). Probably some small number of southern Sindhians were taken into the service after the capture of Dēwal ; then came the levy of 4000 from Sīwastān, and before the Indus was crossed the contagion of defection had spread to Eastern Sindh, and we read of troops supplied to M. Qāsim by the Thākurs of *Bēt*—some district, now unknown, on the left bank of the river. In estimating the strength of the field-army considerable deduction must be made for the detachments garrisoning the principal places taken in Western Sindh. Bilādhurī says that 4000 men were left to garrison Dēwal, but after the reduction of Western Sindh a large portion of this force would no doubt be recalled to the field-army.

[86] It is stated in the Chach Nāma that the Arabs arrived at Dēwal on a Friday in Muharram 73 H. The year is obviously wrong, and should probably be corrected to 92, as the arrival at Ashbhār is said to have occurred in Muharram 93 (Oct.-Nov. 711 A.D.).

perhaps nearly up to Ūmarkot—and so late as the last century the Raos of Kachchh appear to have had garrisons in Badīn, Balhiārī and Rahmaka Bāzār.[87] The Rāsal here referred to is mentioned in the Chach Nāma as one of Prince Dāhir's chiefs. He and his brother, named Moka Bisāya, proved faithless like so many others, and we find M. Qāsim promising to bestow on him the lordship not only of Qaṣṣa, but of Sorath (Kāthīāwār) also. The probability then is that the river was crossed somewhere to the south-east of Nīrūn. A considerable time elapsed before this operation could be effected owing to the Arab force being crippled by the breaking out of the disease called "Juzām" among the horses, large numbers of which were consequently lost. Supplies too seem to have become scarce, and it may be suspected that but for the supineness and weakness of Prince Dāhir and the treason of his chiefs it would have gone hard with the invaders at this period. When at last a bridge of boats was thrown across the river and the army passed over into eastern Sindh, it was able to capture Jaham with comparative ease. Then it moved to a place called *Jēwar*, and afterwards to the vicinity of the fortress of *Rāwar*, which appears to have been situated on a stream called the *Dadhāwāh*, or perhaps *Wadhāwāh*. Outside this fortress Prince Dāhir at last met the invaders, and, after fighting, which is reported to have lasted six days, he was killed and his army routed. The scene of the action is described as "between the Mihrān and the stream called Dadhāwāh," and the date as "Ramzān 93 H," or June 712 A.D. None of these places can now be identified. It may be that Dadhāwāh, or Wadhāwah, represents *Wandanwāh*, or the eastern Nārā (ancient Hākro), *Wandan* having been a name of one portion of that stream in former times. Rāwar must have been some considerable distance from Brahmanābād, as between these places there were two strong fortresses, called *Bahrūr* and *Dhalīla*, which were besieged in succession by the Arabs, and each of which held out for two months against them. Such places cannot have been near one another, and neither can have been near Brahmanābād, which was strongly garrisoned, otherwise the Arabs could not have carried on siege operations for weeks together without some diversion being made against them from the still intact fortresses. Rāwar was pro-

[87] Lieutenant Burnes' Memoir on the Eastern Branch of the Indus in *Transactions of R.A.S.* vol. iii. p. 552.

bably, then, not less than 80 miles from Brahmanābād and perhaps on the Eastern Nārā, in which case it would be about 70 miles south-east of Nīrūm. The place is said in the Chach Nāma to have been founded by Chach and completed by his son Dāhir, who "dwelt there during the four months of the hot season, for the place was pleasant and the climate agreeable." It is also said that he spent the four months of cold weather at Brahmanābād, and the rest of the year at Alor. From these indications it is clear that Rāwar was somewhere in Lower Sindh, where the influence of the sea-breezes renders the climate during the hot season temperate in comparison with that of Central and Upper Sindh.

The further course of the Arab conquest carries us beyond the limits of Lower Sindh, and consequently we part from the Chach Nāma. That chronicle closes with the recall of M. Qāsim on the accession of Sulaymān to the Khilāfat in 715, by which time the young Arab leader had conquered all the Indus territory up to Multān.[88] The Futūhu's-Sind of Bilādhurī continues the history of the Arab relations with Sindh down to the middle of the ninth century. It was a troublous period, marked by the struggles of members of the late reigning family to recover some portion of their lost dominion, by local uprisings, occasioned no doubt by Muslim intolerance and rapacity, and by deeds of treachery and bloodshed among the Arabs themselves. During this period the Arab capital El Mansūra was founded in Central Sindh, and thenceforth contemporary history never mentions ancient Brahmanābād, which was but seven or eight miles distant from the Arab fortress.[89] One incident which occurred in these years may be mentioned, as its scene was evidently in the neighbourhood of the Lower Ḍelta country. It is stated that the Arab governor Junayd (*circa* 724–6) fought a

[88] The story of his end as given in the Chach Nāma is ridiculous fiction. Bilādhurī tells us, what is no doubt quite true, that M. Qāsim, with others of his family, was tortured and put to death by the new governor of 'Irāq, Sālih bin 'Abdu'r-Rahmān (Hajjāj had died in 714), in revenge for the execution of the latter's brother by Hajjāj.

[89] A short paper on the sites of these two places will be found in the *Journal of the R. A. Society*, vol. xvi., Part 2. El Mansūra, according to Bilādhurī, was founded by 'Amr, son of the conqueror of Sindh, and apparently about 730–40. But any son of M. Qāsim, who had hardly arrived at man's estate when he was put to death, *circa* 715 or 716, must have been very young even at the end of the above decade, and it is perhaps more probable that Masūdī and Idrīsī are correct in saying that the Arab capital was built in the beginning of the reign of the 'Abbāside Khalīfa El Mansūr who succeeded in 753–4.

naval battle with Jēsīya, son of the late Prince Dāhir, in what is called the *Baṭīḥatu'sh-Sharqīy*. The root-meaning of "Batīha" is *expanse*, and the word is said by Arab lexicographers to mean "a wide water-course, or channel of a torrent." (Lane, sub. rad. بطح) In a modern map I have seen it applied to the swamps on the west of the Shaṭṭu'l Arab in 'Irāq, and I feel no doubt that in the present case Baṭīḥatu'sh-Sharqīy means the *eastern inland sea*, that is, the sea that once permanently covered, and that still periodically covers, the Ran of Kachchh. As we do not know at what season of the year this action was fought, we cannot deduce from the fact of its occurrence that the Ran was still permanently under water in the eighth century. There might have been a battle between two fleets of boats there in July or August while during the other months of the year the Ran might be quite dry. How such an action came about is intelligible enough. Jēsīya had no doubt been collecting troops in Kachchh, which was then a province of Sindh, for purposes of aggression on the Indus territory, and Junayd probably attacked him while he was transporting them across the Ran. In this fight Jēsīya was taken prisoner and killed. His brother Chach (so called, no doubt, after his grandfather, the founder of the line), whom Arabs named Ṣaṣṣa, fled to 'Irāq to lay his case before the Khalīfa, but on his return he was beguiled into a meeting with Junayd who had him killed. So ended the Brahman dynasty of Sindh.

V.

EASTERN GEOGRAPHERS ON CENTRAL AND LOWER SINDH.

Most of what is interesting in the writings of the eastern geographers on Lower Sindh has already come under notice in connection with the identification of Dēwal and Nīrūn. It remains to refer to a few places of minor importance which are mentioned in their works. The geographers who bore respectively the surnames of Istakhrī, Ibnu Hawqil and El Masūdī appear to have visited Sindh themselves at some time in the first half of the tenth century. Little information, unfortunately, is to be gained from them in regard to the courses of the Indus and its branches in their time. Geography, in their view, was very much a mere matter of the topography of the principal towns of a country and the laying down of itineraries. What is recorded too is not always independent work, and one copies from another with little discrimination or care to check a previous account by the result of his own personal observation. Very much too of their labour has lost its value in consequence of the corruptions—inevitable where the Arabic character is employed, unless extreme care be taken first by the author and then by the transcriber—which have crept into the texts, rendering it a hopeless task to guess at the actual names represented by combinations of incomplete or distorted letters.

In the itineraries distance is measured by the "day's journey," though occasionally the "farsang" (in Persian "farsakh") is substituted. It may be worth while to attempt to ascertain what approximation to definite value may be assigned to so vague a standard, and for this purpose to compare the more accurately determined, or estimated, distances of modern times with those laid down by the old geographers in the case of places which can be identified either with absolute certainty or a near approach to it. The following routes are taken from an itinerary of Istak͟hrī, some of the places being in Makrān and Las, others in modern Sindh. It may be mentioned that Kīz is certainly identifiable with Kēj; that Armābil was close to Las Bēla (perhaps two or three miles to the west of it); that Kanbalī must have been on, or close to, the site of Son Mīānī, and that Manhātar must have been somewhere in the vicinity of Karāchī.

	Distances according to Istakhri.	Distances according to modern routes, ascertained mileage, or map-measurement.	Average miles per diem.
	Days.	Miles.	
1. Kīz to Armābīl	6	230	38
2. Armābīl to Kanbalī	2	70	35
3. Kanbalī to Manhātar[90]	2	52	26
4. Manhātar to Dēwal	2	46	23
5. Dēwal to Nīrūn	4	87	22
6. Nīrūn to Manṣūra	2	46	23
7. Sadūsān to Manjābari	3	66	22
8. Manṣūra to Alor	7	160 (about)	23

The first two routes in this list show exceedingly long stages, and

[90] Manhātar is omitted by Istak͟hrī, but is mentioned by Ibnu Hawqil and El Idrisi, who calls it *Manhābarī*.

it may be suspected that in the first, at all events, some error has occurred. At the present day, I imagine, it would be considered fairly fast travelling to go from Kēj to Las Bēla in twice the time mentioned by Istakhrī. Of course the nature of the country traversed would be an important factor in determining the general length of stages. The comparative abundance or scarcity of convenient halting places would cause the standard of the "day's journey" to vary considerably in different districts or provinces, a fact which the old writers who used that standard left out of account in drawing up their itineraries. In Sindh, as far as we can judge from the routes above given, the standard was very uniform, owing, no doubt, to the considerable number of towns and villages along the river, or at no great distance from it, a circumstance which would permit of stages being made of moderate length, and of the number of hours devoted to travelling being generally about the same every day.

The only place in the Delta country besides Dēwal and Nīrūn mentioned by the eastern geographers is Manhātar. The compiler Idrīsī calls this place Manhābarī, and has consequently led himself and others into confusion about it. General Cunningham identifies it with Ṭhaṭa, and the Indo-Scythian capital Minnagar. ("An. Geog. of India," pp. 288 ff). He says: "Manhābarī is described by all the authorities as situated on the western bank of the Indus at 2 days' journey from Dēbal. Now this is the very position of Thatha, which is on the western bank of the Indus at 40 miles, or 2 days' journey from Lārī-bandar, which was almost certainly within a few miles of the famous city of Dēbal." He goes on to suggest that for *Manhābarī* "we might perhaps read *Mandābarī*, the city of the Mand tribe," and as this tribal name is variously written as *Mer*, *Med*, *Mand*, and *Mind*, Mandābarī may be the "city of the Mins, that is Minnagar." Unfortunately for all this reasoning, and much more on the same subject which it is not necessary to quote, Manhābarī, though, according to the geographer cited by General Cunningham, to the west of the Mihrān, and 2 days' journey from Dēbal, was 2 days *west* of that place, and consequently, accepting General Cunningham's own identification of Dēbal, Manhābarī was fully 80 miles west of Ṭhaṭa. Idrīsī blundered about this place owing to Manhātar and Manjābarī reading so much alike in the Arabic character, but General Cunningham quotes from him only so much as seems to support his Minnagar theory, and omits what conclusively disproves it. Idrīsī says: "From Sharūsān (Sēwan̲) to Manhābarī (here Manjābarī should be read), a town, placed in a hollow, well built, of a pleasant aspect, surrounded with gardens, fountains and running waters, *the distance is 3 days.* From the latter place to Fīrabūz (in Mekrān) 6 days. (Here he confuses Manjābarī with Manhātār). From Manhābarī (read Manhātār) to Dēbal 2 days. In going from Dēbal to Fīrabūz the road passes by Manhābarī (Manhātār), &c." It is quite clear that a Manhābarī which was only 3 days, or about 66 miles from Sēwan̲, cannot possibly be identified with Ṭhaṭa, which is at a distance of 140 miles from that place; also that a Manhābarī which was on the bank of the Mihrān cannot be identical with a Manhābarī which was 40 miles west of Dēwal, let the site of that port be placed where it may. Thus the attempted identification of Minnagar falls to the ground.

The Manhātar of Ibnu Hawqil was evidently somewhere in the neighbourhood of Karāchī, since it was 2 days from Dēwal, on the road to Mekrān. If the final syllable of the name is genuine, and not a corruption, it may indicate that Manhātar was a small seaport, *tar* being a Sindhi word for a landing-place, and its site may have been the Observatory island which has been mentioned in an earlier part of this memoir (p. 13). This, however, would place it rather too far from the road between Mekrān and Sindh, and a more likely situation would be somewhere on the Līārī, where the "Government Gardens" now are, and close to the road from Karāchī to the Hab river and thence on to Son Miānī, Las Bēla and Mekrān, which has little, if at all, varied from time immemorial.

Manjābarī, again, was a place of which the position can be fixed within a mile or two. It was on the western bank of the Mihrān (the Luhāno channel), 3 days from Sēwan̲ and 2 days from Nīrūn. "Manjābarī (says Ibnu Hawqil) is to the west of the Mihrān, and there any one who proceeds from Dēbal to Manṣūra will have to pass the river, the latter place being *opposite to Manjābarī.*" The site then may be approximately fixed about 8 miles south-east of the modern Shahdādpur, and on the west bank of the still extant and clearly defined Luhāno channel. There can be no doubt whatever that in the tenth century the river was flowing through this channel. Both what is said of Manjābarī and of Manṣūra by the geographers of that time make this quite clear. As to the course farther north we are left very much to conjecture and to a choice between the various channels that can still be distinctly traced through the Pargana of Sakarand and thence northward to Alor. There is a town named by the geographers as situated to the north of Manṣūra which, if we could discover its site, would guide us with certainty to the course of the Indus in this part of Sindh at the time referred to. This is *Kalrī*, which is sometimes written Kalarī and Kālarī, and sometimes appears in still more corrupt forms in the works of the old geographers. As *Kalro* and *Kalrī* are not uncommon place-names in Sindh, it is safe to assume that the latter is the correct name in this case. Of this place Idrīsī says: "Kālarī, upon the west bank of the Mihrān, is a pretty town, well fortified, and is a busy trading place. Near it the Mihrān separates into two branches; the largest runs towards the west as far as the city of Mansūria, which is on the west bank; the other runs towards the north-west, then to the north and then towards the west. Both again unite at the distance of about 12 miles below Mansūria. Although this town is some distance out of the regular route, still it is much frequented in consequence of the profitable trade carried on with the inhabitants. From hence to Mansūria is a hard day's journey of 40 miles; from Kālarì to Sharūsān (Sēwan̲) 3 days" (Elliot, I. 79). There is much in this description which is absurd. The Indus is represented as running for a long distance from south to north, that is to say, *against* the fall of the country. But it is no unusual slip among writers of all ages and countries to exactly reverse the cardinal points when indicating a bearing, and if we suppose that to have been done in the present case and make the necessary corrections, the course of the river as described will become intelligible, but the description will now be found inconsistent with the writer's statement in another place that the river ran from Kālarī towards Sēwan̲. Further, the expression used by Istak̲h̲rī and Ibnu Hawqil that Manṣūra was surrounded by a *K̲h̲alīj* from the river, implies that the capital was not on the main stream but on a branch, and the maps of both writers plainly indicate that such was the case.[91] The distance from Kālarī to Manṣūra is said to be "a hard day's journey of 40 miles." Idrīsī, however, employed the "farsang," not the mile, to express

[91] *Khalīj* may mean either an artificial channel, or a natural *branch* stream. When there is mention of more than one channel *K̲h̲alīj* would apply to an inferior one. (Lane, Lex, s.r. خلج.)

distances, and his French translator, extracts from whose work have been rendered into English for Elliot's History, seems to have assumed a value of 4 miles for the farsang, whereas it is probable from the fact of the journey, though long, being accomplished in one day, that Idrīsī's "farsang" was the smaller one of 3 miles; and 10 "farsangs" of this value would be a sufficiently "hard" day's journey. Now just at this distance of 30 miles north-west of the site of Manṣūra (the present so-called Brahmanābād) and 10 miles north-east of the town of Sakarand, there is a township bearing the name of Kalrī. Somewhere in this neighbourhood the flourishing commercial town described by the old geographers may have been situated. The tract of country is furrowed with long abandoned channels running from north to south, or from north-west to south-east, showing where the Indus once flowed at distances sometimes exceeding 20 miles east of its present course. And along these channels the land is strewn with the broken brick and pottery, so familiar to the traveller in Sindh, which mark the sites of once flourishing towns and villages. There is thus everything to favour the conjecture that the Kālarī of the eastern geographers was in this district. Here, however, it would not be 3 days' journey from Sēwan̠ as asserted by Idrīsī, nor is it possible to place its site at any point on any conceivable course of the Mihrān where it would be at the same time 3 days from Sēwan̠ and a "hard day's journey" above Manṣūra. The probability is that Idrīsī confounded the distance between the two places with that which he found recorded as between Sēwan̠ and Manjābarī. It seems too that while Ibnu Hawqil says Kālarī was on the west of the Mihrān, in which he is followed by Idrīsī, the place was really to the east of the river. At least so it appears in both Ibnu Hawqil's and Istākhrī's maps.[92] From somewhere near this point, then, a branch stream issued from the Indus on the left bank, and, flowing south-east, passed round the walls of Mansūra on the east side and then, turning south-westward, rejoined the main river at a spot about 3 farsangs,

[92] In my paper on the sites of Brahmanābād and Manṣūra in the *Journal of the R. A. Society*, I suggested that the *K̲halīj* which surrounded Mansūra was a canal which had been led from the Luhāno channel at a point much lower down the river than the probable site of the Kalrī referred to in the text. That point is in a township named *Kalro*, a fact which had some part in leading me to adopt the suggestion of the canal to which, on further consideration, I cannot adhere. The distance from Kalrī to Manṣūra, which can hardly have been less than thirty miles, is a fatal objection to the canal suggestion, and by *K̲halīj* I now believe a natural channel was intended.

or, say, 9 miles from the capital. Of the bed of this branch stream there is a remnant at Manṣūra itself, but probably other traces of it might be found farther to the north-west.

There is one more point connected with the course of the Indus in Central Sindh in the tenth century which may be noticed in concluding this section. Ibnu Hawqil says: "He who travels from Manṣūra to Buddha must go along the banks of the Mihrān as far as the city of Sadūstān (Sēwan̲). From this it would naturally be inferred that when the geographer was in Sindh the Indus was flowing close by Sēwan̲; and such may have been the case, though it would not be safe, considering the utter absence of precision in these old writers, to conclude that the simple statement here quoted conveys an accurate idea of the course of the river at that time. It would have been quite in accordance with the geographer's loose method to make that statement, though the river were in fact 10 or 12 miles to the east of Sēwan̲ when he was in Sindh. It may, for instance, have been the case that the route from the Arab capital to the principal town of Western Sindh was along the Indus as far as the mouth of the Aral, and thence along the latter stream to Sēwan̲. In the Chach Nāma various branch streams of the Indus are mentioned, as the *Aral*, the *Dadhāwāh*, the *Kotak* (or *Kotal*), the *Manjhal*, the *Jalwātī*, the *Barṭarī*,[93] of which only the first is now in existence, while of none of the others can the channels be identified; but of any branch stream, with the exception of that which flowed by Manṣūra, we get no hint from the old geographers, and Ibnu Hawqil may not have thought it worth while to mention that part of the route to Sēwan̲ lay along the Aral.

[93] This name is of interest. Burton, I think, says somewhere that Hindus call the Shrine at Sēwan̲, known to the Muhammedans as *Lāl Shāhbāz*, *Rājā Bartārī*, which no doubt represents *Bharṭriharī*, the name of the prince-ascetic, and brother of King Vikramāditya, who lived in the last century before the Christian era. Colonel Tod says in his "Rājāsthān" (I. 776), that Bhartriharī is reported to have lived for a time at Sēwan̲, on the Indus, and no doubt the fame of so great a devotee would be widespread in Sindh as it was in all northern India. The name is spelt برطري the ط being probably intended to represent the Sanscrit ऋ in Bharṭriharī.

VI.

THE DELTA COUNTRY AFTER THE SECOND MUHAMMEDAN INVASION OF INDIA.

As the power of the Abbāside Khalīfas declined, and troubles at the heart of their dominion more and more absorbed the attention and taxed the resources of the rulers at Baghdād, the outlying provinces of the Khilāfat gradually fell off from their obedience. The Indus territory, which had been divided into the two provinces of Multān and Manṣūra, the latter nearly corresponding with the Sindh of the present day, became independent, the governor of each setting up as sovereign where he had lately ruled as vassal. This state of things endured till the invasions of the great Mahmūd in the early years of the eleventh century gave the first shock to pretensions which were ultimately extinguished by his successors in Ghaznī and India. Meanwhile the Arab capital in Central Sindh ceased to be the seat of power on the Lower Indus, and gave place to Bakhar. Alor appears to have been abandoned owing to a change in the course of the Indus, by which the old Hindu capital lost its water supply; and it is probable that the depopulation of Manṣūra was due to the same cause. Apart from local legends connected with *Dalu Rāe*, a prince who occupies a doubtful position in the borderland between history and legend, Alor is not heard of after the middle of the tenth century—the period of the Arab geographers; and "ancient Brahmanābād" disappears from history during the rule of the early Arab governors. Manṣūra, founded, as we have seen, probably soon after the middle of the eighth century, had a comparatively short life. It is spoken of by Yāqūt, who wrote his great geographical work in the second decade of the thirteenth century, as if it was still flourishing; but Ebu'l-Fidā, writing in the first half of the fourteenth century, says that the city, with three others of the same name in different parts of the East, was then in ruins. If both writers were correct, it is probably to be inferred that a great change in the course of the Indus took place at some time between the middle of the thirteenth and the early years of the fourteenth century, and caused the ruin of Mansūra.

In Lower Sindh, a part of the province which, owing to its distance from the new centres of Muhammedan power, and perhaps to its being held of small value, was long left in a state of partial independence, a native tribe, named *Sūmra,* contrived to gain a position of supremacy about the middle of the eleventh century A.D.; and its chiefs claimed, and for long periods together actually exercised, sovereign authority in the Delta country east of the Indus during the greater part of three centuries. The Sūmra are known to be a Rājput tribe, though, since the conversion of the great body of the Sindhian branch to Islām, Muhammedan pride and imagination have discovered an Arab origin for them. The determination of the precise period of their emerging from obscurity and of their fall from power has always been a crucial difficulty in the history of Sindh. Sir H. Elliot calls it "one of the most difficult problems with which we have to deal in the history of Muhammedan India" (Hist. I. App. 483). Yet we are not without some data of reasonably satisfactory character to guide us to a settlement of the question. Mīr M'aṣūm of Bakhar, in his history of Sindh (Tārīkh-i-Sind, finished 1600 A.D.) says the Sūmra seized upon authority in Lower Sindh in the reign of Abdu'r-Rashīd, son of the great Mahmūd. This prince came to the throne in 441 H. or 1049–50 A.D., and reigned only 2½ years. It is matter of veritable history that he was of weak and indolent character, and that as a consequence of his feebleness disorders and rebellion broke out in the more distant provinces of his kingdom. There is, then, much in favour of the probability that Mir M'aṣūm's statement is correct. Some further evidence has been supplied by a local chronicle in Kachchh which, so far as I know, has never hitherto been noticed in connection with this question. Colonel Tod, in his "Travels in Western India" (p. 470), mentions an old chronicle of Ghūmlī in Kachchh in which it is stated that the time of Jām Ūnar's succession was about 1053 A.D., and that the *Samās* became Musulmāns at this period. Now the chronicle is here clearly mixing up Sūmras and Samās, and confounding *Ūmar* with *Ūnar.* Jām Ūnar was the first of the *Samā* line of princes, and there is evidence to show that the Samās did not supplant the Sūmras till the twelfth century; before which time there is reason to believe there was no general conversion of the Samās to Islām. But I have no doubt that the chronicler recorded what was currently accepted in Sindh and the neighbouring countries as the approximate date of so noteworthy an event as the sudden rise of a tribal chief to princely power; though his acquaintance with the real history of the two tribes was not accurate enough to keep him from blundering on other points. The same year is assigned also by another writer, Md. Yūsuf, whom Elliot (I. App, 485) mentions, as that of the beginning of Sūmra rule. It seems to me that this evidence is sufficient. Nothing could be more likely than that an outlying portion of the Ghaznavide dominions, such as Lower Sindh, should take advantage of the sovereign's weakness to assert its independence. This would not happen immediately on the accession of the sovereign, nor until there had been time for it to become generally known throughout his dominions that his character was of a kind to make rebellion a safe venture. Thus as 'Abdu'r-Rashīd came to the throne in 1050, a date of some three years later is an extremely probable one for the Sūmra rising. I assume then that in the year 1053 A.D. we have the *terminus a quo* which we are seeking, and it remains to ascertain the *terminus ad quem*—the date of the overthrow of Sūmra authority. Mīr M'aṣūm, whose account of the Sūmra and Samā periods is the most detailed of any that has come down to us, is greatly defective in the matter of dates, and it is only when we come upon some point of contact between local and imperial history that we can feel ourselves on anything like firm ground in regard to chronology. The events which accompanied the accession of Ūnar, the first Samā prince of Lower Sindh, are narrated by Mīr M'aṣūm but without a single date. Most fortunately a foreign traveller, coming from as far west as the Pillars of Hercules, arrived in Sindh "just after," as he himself says, these same events, which he too describes but in much more detail than Mīr M'aṣūm; and through him we are able to fix the date of the close of Sūmra rule, and the accession of the first Samā prince, with some precision in the year 1333 A.D.[94] Thus the entire period of Sūmra supremacy was 280 years. In regard to the number of princes who held sway during this period there is considerable diversity of statement by the historians, but the question is of little interest compared with the broader one of the length of time through which the mastery of a single line of tribal

[94] The case is more fully treated in a paper on "Ibnu Baṭūṭa in Sindh," in the *R.A.S. Journal*, vol. xix., Part 3. The "Beg-Lār Nāma," a local history written in the early part of the seventeenth century, gives the year 734 H. (1333–34 A.D.) as the first of the Samā rule, though the author had probably never heard of Ibnu Baṭūṭa.

chiefs endured. The late Mr. E. Thomas has shown that the average duration of reign in the case of Indian sovereigns should be taken at about 17 years.[95] Applying this average in the case of the Sūmras we get a total number of 16 or 17 princes, and it becomes pretty certain that Mīr M'aṣūm is wrong in putting the number at 12, which would give an average reign of over 23 years. On the other hand the Tuḥfatū'l-Kirām, a local history composed in the eighteenth century, has probably stumbled on the truth when stating the number of princes to have been seventeen; though the author would have been more prudent if he had avoided the temptation of giving the length of each reign (except in two instances) with the result of bringing the total Sūmra period up to some 370 years, with an average reign of nearly 22 years.

The first seat of Sūmra power was the town of *Ṭharī*. There is more than one place of this name in Lower Sindh, but the Sūmra capital was most probably in the Ṭharī township on the right bank of the Western Purān, where the ruins of an old town still exist about 6½ miles east by south from the present Muhabbat Dēro. In the India Office copy of Mīr M'aṣūm's history, and also in the Sindhī version, Ṭharī is in one place described as "on the bank of the river," meaning, of course, the Purān, and it may be that in early Sūmra times that branch of the Indus was still flowing. Later in those times the first capital was abandoned in favour of *Tūr*, on a branch of the Indus now called the *Gūngro*. Why the change was made is not known, but it may have been in consequence of the drying-up of the Western Purān. The ruins of Tūr are to be seen at a spot 28 miles east of Ṭhaṭa, near the village of Shāh Kapur.[96] "Not I alone but many others have beheld these ruins with astonishment," says the author of the local history called the "Tārīkh-i-Tāhirī." The second capital of the Sūmras appears, indeed, to have been the finest city in all Sindh. It was situated on the south, or left, bank of the Gūngro, the upper course of which it is now difficult to trace, but it would appear, so far as the channel can be observed, to have issued from the Rēn. According to the Tuḥfatū'l-Kirām Tūr was destroyed by the troops of 'Alā'u'd-Dīn Khaljī. This is extremely probable, and the event, no doubt, occurred about the end of the

[95] See his paper on the "Sah Kings" (p. 36 note).

[96] An article on these ruins by Captain (now Major-General) Phillips was published in the Journal of the Bombay Branch R.A.S., about 35 years ago.

thirteenth century, or early in the following one. The pretensions of the chiefs of Lower Sindh to independence were never for a moment admitted at Delhi, and the destruction of their capital was likely enough to be 'Alā'u'd-Dīn's way of reading a practical lesson on the real facts of their situation to the presumptuous Sūmras. A few years later the Samās of Kachchh and Lower Sindh seized upon authority, and, following the example of their predecessors, assumed to be independent of any overlord. This happened, as we have seen, about 1333 A.D.

The Sūmra chiefs seem to have confined themselves to the Eastern Delta country; that is to say, their western boundary coincided pretty nearly with the present course of the Indus in the Delta. The Samā rulers, on acquiring power, passed beyond this limit, and one of their first acts was the founding of a new capital at a spot below the northern end of the low ridge of hills which runs due south from the Kalrī to the Baghār, a distance of 15 miles. The site selected was on the southern, or left, bank of the Kalrī, and the new capital was named *Sāmū-ī*. At the same time, or soon afterwards, the fort of *Tughlaqābād*, now known as *Kalā-Koṭ*, was founded, or perhaps only restored, 6 miles south of Sāmū-ī on the ridge of hills just mentioned. The author of the "Tuhfatu'l-Kirām" says that "when Tūr was destroyed by the troops of 'Alā'u'd-Dīn, and the Sūmras gave place to the Samās, the ancient and ruined fort and city, named from *Rājā Kalā*, *Kalā-Kot*, became the capital and received the name of Tughlaqābād from Jām Tughlaq"; and he adds that "neither Sāmū-ī nor Tughlaqābād was finished, when, space being insufficient (at Sāmū-ī), Ṭhaṭa was founded and made the capital."[97] The local historians were in the habit of speaking of Ṭhaṭa as if it had been in existence long years before it was actually founded, and of sometimes applying the name not only to the city but to all Lower Sindh. Hence, as well as from real ignorance of facts, much confusion prevails about the date of the foundation of the Samā capital, and it may be well to see what evidence on the point is to be gathered from other sources. Ibnu Baṭūṭa, who must have passed

[97] The founding, or restoration, of Kalā-Koṭ must have taken place long before Jām Tughlaq's time, for he (according to Mīr M'aṣūm) was the twelfth of the Samā princes, and the building of the fortress is represented as coincident with the rise of the Samās. The names of *Kalān*-Kot or "Great Fort," and *Kalyān*-Koṭ, or "Beautiful Fort," are corruptions introduced by English writers, and are unknown to natives.

close to the sites of Sāmū-ī and Ṭhaṭa when sailing down the Indus from Sēwan to Lāhorī Bandar in 1334 A.D., makes no mention of either. Both, however, might have then been in existence, but not as yet large enough to attract much attention from a traveller. It is noticeable, too, that Ibnu Baṭūṭa mentions only those towns in Sindh at which he stayed for a time, and the result is that only four towns are named by him. If we turn to histories of India, we find, so far as I know, no mention of Ṭhaṭa before the year 1347 A.D., or thereabouts. The "Tarīkh-i-Fīrūz-shāhī" of Barnī mentions it then for the first time when narrating the circumstances of the rebellion in Guzerat got up by the cobbler Taghī; and it must be remembered that the author was writing contemporary history, and that he actually accompanied Muhammed Shāh to Sindh, and nearly to Ṭhaṭa itself, in the expedition which was intended to put an end to the cobbler, but put an end to the Sultan instead. Taking this evidence together with the fact of the foundation of Ṭhaṭa being ascribed by the local historians to the very first years of Samā rule, and allowing a few years for the interval spent in the partial construction of Sāmū-ī, it is probably safe to place the building of the Samā capital approximately in the year 1340 A.D., or the Hijra year 741–42. It is clear, in any case, that the vulgar belief that Thata owes its origin to Nizāmu'd-Din, better known as Jām Nanda, who succeeded in 866 H., or 1461–62 A.D., is absurdly opposed to historical facts.

In regard to the hydrography of the Western Delta at this time, all that we can gather with any degree of certainty is that the Kalrī must have been a perennial stream, or the Samās would not have chosen a site for their chief town on its bank. Two centuries later, as we shall see hereafter, this channel carried the main body of the Indus, and it was very likely the principal channel when Ṭhaṭa was founded. It seems probable, from the remains of abandoned channels existing in the neighbourhood, that a bifurcation of the river took place 8 to 12 miles north-east of Ṭhaṭa, whence the Baghār or Dēwal stream, flowed south-west, leaving the new capital a short distance from its right bank, and going on to the sea by the present channel. A little eastward of the spot which I consider to be the site of Dēwal this stream was joined by the Kalrī, and thus Ṭhaṭa, with an oblong tract of country some hundreds of square miles in extent, was completely insulated.

At this period Dēwal was no longer heard of. We know from Ibnu Baṭūṭa that *Lāharī* was now the Delta port. This place situated on the *Rāho* channel, a mere prolongation of the Baghār, is very ancient, and, in respect of its duration as the port of the Delta, probably rivals Dēwal itself. It is first mentioned by El Birūnī early in the eleventh century, and it was abandoned in consequence of the Rāho becoming too shoal for sea-going vessels, at the end of the eighteenth century. It had two names, *Lāharī* and *Lāhorī*, the close resemblance between which might cause it to be supposed that one was a slight corruption of the other; but such, I believe, was not the case. El Birūnī calls the port *Lohārānī*, which is equivalent to the later Lāhorī; for *Lohāwar* was the ancient name of the capital of the Punjāb and the only one known to El Birūnī. Lohāwarānī, or Lohārānī, as it would probably be pronounced in common speech, was thus a name indicating the connection between the port and the capital; and as in course of time Lohāwar became Lāhor, so the name of the port was transformed from Lohārānī to Lāhorī. The justification of the name lay in the fact that Lāharī was the port of the Panjab as well as of Sindh; the Indus and its affluents being among the grand trade-routes marked out by Nature for mankind, and followed from the very beginnings of external commerce. As to the importance of the trade that followed this route at the comparatively late period of three centuries ago, we have the following statement from the journal of two Englishmen, Richard Steele and John Crowther, on their way from Ājmīr to Ispahān in 1614. "Lahore is a goodly great citie, and one of the fairest and ancientest of India. . . . . From this place came the treasure (the best) of the Portugals' trade, when they had peace, as being the centre of all Indian traffique. And here they embarqued the same downe the riuer for Tatta whence they were transported for Ormus and Persia. The merchants also passing that way betwixt Persia and India payd them fraight. They did likewise driue a great trade up the riuer for pepper and spices, furnishing these parts of India therewith."[98] Thus we have from a modern source an indirect but very unmistakable explanation of the origin of the place-name Lohārānī, Lāhorī. But this would be the name by which the part was known outside of Sindh in northern India. The indigenous name was

[98] "Purchas' Pilgrims" (I. 520). I imagine that this trade was carried on by the Portuguese principally by means of native factors at Lāhor and Ṭhaṭa.

Lāhaṟī, which it had from the tribe of *Lāhaṟ* settled in that part of the Delta, and said to be still represented there, whose occupation was boating and seafaring, combined, perhaps, with the less legitimate pursuits of coast tribes whenever the hand of a strong government was not present to restrain them. When Englishmen first visited the Indus Delta they called this port "*the City Diul*"—an echo of ancient Dēwal which they had caught from the Portuguese—and "*Larrybunder*," their own version of the indigenous name.

The Samā tribe, like the Sūmra, both of which are still numerous in Sindh, almost all being now Musulmāns, was originally Rājput, and had been settled for centuries in the Lower Indus valley before their chiefs acquired princely power in Southern Sindh. The northern Samā are mentioned in the Chach Nāma in the early time of Rāe Chach in the first half of the seventh century, when they occupied, as their descendants do largely still, the tract of country now known as the Kandhiāro Pargana. Those with whom we are now concerned were the southern Samā, who were first settled in Kac̲h̲c̲h̲h and afterwards spread over the Delta country. Their history, after they rose to a dominating position, is of much more interest than that of the Sūmra, for they early came into collision with the Imperial Government, and, down almost to the close of their period of power, displayed a remarkable fighting capacity and ability to hold their own in what might have been thought an utterly hopeless struggle for independence. Another fact which gives interest to their time is the conversion of great numbers, perhaps of the majority, of the people from Hinduism to Islām. How this came about—through what immediate influence—is not known, but the movement seems to have been sudden and the process short. The names of the Sūmra chiefs which have been recorded are all Hindū. The first Samā prince, or *Jām*, as they came now to be called, was, according to Ibnu Baṭūṭa, a Muhammedan, though his name, Ūnar, as his father's, Bābūnī, was Hindū. This indicates a recent conversion. The son of Tamāchī, the third prince of the line, was carried a prisoner to Delhi while still a child, and when, after long captivity, he was released, he returned to Sindh with a distinctly Muhammedan name—Khayru'd-Dīn. Perhaps it had been pointed out at Delhi that though in Sindh, where conversion had but recently begun to make headway among the people, the practice of

Musulmans bearing Hindu names might be tolerated, it was "bad form" to continue it at the capital. Two of Khayru'd-Dīn's sons succeeded to the Sindh throne, and both bore Hindū names, Bābūnī and Tamāchī, but after them the dynasty became strictly orthodox in this matter.

Khayru'd-Dīn appears to have come back from Delhi with anything but a friendly feeling for the master who had restored him to liberty and honour, but claimed his allegiance to the imperial throne. In his time occurred the rebellion in Guzerat which has been already mentioned, and Khayru'd-Dīn gave the cobbler an asylum and defied the Sultan. When the latter died near Ṭhaṭa his nephew and successor, Fīrūz Shāh, with an army completely demoralised and his uncle's Mughal allies actually assailing him and plundering his camp, found himself compelled to abandon the expedition and retreat northwards. This was the signal for Khayru'd-Dīn to assume the offensive. He fell upon the rear of the imperialists and harassed the retreat as far as the town of *San*, a distance of 100 miles from Ṭhaṭa. The disgraceful collapse of the expedition and the crowning humiliation inflicted by Khayru'd-Dīn rankled in the breast of Firūz Shah. Eight years later he returned to take vengeance on the Samā prince, but only accomplished his purpose after failure in a first campaign and coming near to perishing with the remnant of his army in retreating across the burning and waterless sands of the Ran of Kachchh.

It is evident from the record of Fīrūz Shāh's second campaign in Sindh, contained in the Tārīkh-i-Firūz Shāhī of Shams-i-Sirāj, that Islām had made great progress in Sindh by that time (about 1361–2 A.D.); that is to say, within 30 years from the accession of the Samās. In that history we are told that the imperial troops captured 4000 of the peasantry in the Eastern Delta country, and "*as they were all Musulmāns*" the Sultan forbade their being made slaves and directed that they should be kindly treated (Elliot, III. 330, 331). That Lower Sindh was then well populated and that the resources of the Samā princes were considerable, appears from another statement of the historian just quoted, to the effect that the villages on the east side of the river were numerous, while it is shown that the imperial force was well subsisted there for several months. The Samā army is put at 20,000 horse and 40,000 foot.[29] This absurd exaggeration

[29] Elliot's copy appears to have had "400,000 infantry!" This must have been due to an error in transcription.

of the historian was no doubt designed to mitigate the shame of Firūz Shah's first failures, and also to enhance the merit of his ultimate success. There can, however, be little question that the long and stubborn resistance offered to the imperial arms indicates that the Samā troops were numerous enough, as they certainly were spirited enough, to entitle them to be considered formidable. Thus the imperial army, though said to be of considerable strength and supplied in great abundance with warlike material, was unable to cross the Indus in Lower Sindh owing to the vigilance and gallant resistance of the Samās. "After much examination and exertion" (says the historian, obliged in spite of his courtly bias to confess the truth) "the transit was found to be impracticable"; and he goes on to state, what is well nigh incredible, that the Sultan actually detached a large part of his army (then near Ṭhaṭa) in feigned retreat as far as Bakhar, where it crossed the river and then descended the right bank to Ṭhaṭa. There, outside the city, it encountered the Samās and, it is very evident, was defeated. The fact comes out as clearly from the historian's ludicrous endeavour to disguise it as if he had frankly admitted the unpleasant truth. This is his description of the affair: "Sultan Firoz was a very cautious man. The fort of Ṭhaṭa was visible (from his position on the left bank), but from the great breadth of the stream the land on the opposite side was not discernible. Therefore it could not be seen how the fight progressed. Sultan Firoz stood watching in expectation, his eyes now lifted to heaven, and now strained over the river in order to learn what was passing. By divine inspiration he sent a trusty man across the river in a boat with orders directing his forces to desist from battle and return to him. *The combatants on both sides were Musulmāns, and if the fighting went on many innocent persons would be slain.* They were accordingly directed to return by the same way they had gone. When the messenger delivered these commands to 'Imādu'l-Mulk and Zafar Khān they retreated with their whole force—marching the 120 *kos* up the farther, or Ṭhaṭa, side of the river to Bakhar where they crossed back and rejoined the main army. The Sultan then said to 'Imādu'l-Mulk, 'Where can this handful of Thatians fly to, unless they creep into an ant-hole like a snake. My army shall remain here and we will build a large city'" (Elliot, III. 331, 332). It is to be hoped that this vulgar and childish disparagement of the stout Samās, who had just beaten the imperialists in a fair field, was the invention of the historian and not really the utterance of the humbled Sultan. The imperial forces had now failed in three successive campaigns against the Samās. Fīrūz Shāh was obliged to send to Delhi for reinforcements, and meanwhile to remain ingloriously inactive in Lower Sindh. But now dissensions broke out in Ṭhaṭa; and though, fortunately for Fīrūz Shāh, supplies were fairly abundant in the Eastern Delta, the country west of the river was exhausted. Famine and discord together did for the Sultan what his own utmost efforts had failed to accomplish. To his great delight the Samā prince surrendered. Khayru'd-Dīn was taken to Delhi, but his brother remained and carried on the government in quasi-obedience to imperial authority.

The anarchy that prevailed at Delhi during the declining years of Fīrūz Shāh, and in the time of his immediate successors, together with the distraction caused by the invasion of Tīmūr's Mughals in 1398, left the Samā rulers a free hand in Sindh, and they seem to have used the independence thus regained with no inconsiderable degree of vigour and political ability. In this respect the Samās had from the first shown themselves greatly superior to their Sūmra predecessors. The author of the "Tārīkh-i-Tāhirī" says of them: "Other towns and villages (besides Sāmū-ī and Tughlaqābād) still flourishing, were built by them. . . . . Lands hitherto barren were now carefully cultivated; there was hardly a span of ground untilled. The divisions into *sūbas* and *parganas*, which are maintained to the present day in the province of Ṭhaṭa, were made by these people" (Elliot, I. 272).

The Samā princes gradually extended their authority over all Sindh; the dynasty reaching the summit of its fame in the time of Nizāmu'd-Dīn, better known as Jām Nanda. This prince, the last but one of his line, succeeded, according to Mīr M'aṣūm, on the 25 Rabi I. 866 H. (3rd Dec. 1461), and reigned 48 years. Mīr M'aṣūm calls him the son of Bābūnī. This was an ancestral name, having been that of the father of the first prince, and also that of the fifth prince. It is, however, rather singular to find Hindū names retained so long after the Samās had become Muhammedan, especially when there are indications that the descendants of the converts were becoming ashamed of bearing such names. On Jām Nanda's tomb at Ṭhaṭa there is an inscription in which he is called the son of Sadru'd-Dīn. This was probably the Muhammedan *alias* by which the father was known, and which alone was considered fitting to inscribe on the son's tomb. The inscription does not contain the date of Jām Nanda's death, but only that of the laying the foundation of the tomb which was 915 H. or 1509 A.D. Thus it is probable that the death took place about the end of 914 H., and Mīr M'asūm's statement that Jām Nanda succeeded in 866 H. and reigned 48 years is most probably correct.[100]

The reign of this prince was the golden age of native rule in Sindh. The fact that his name, alone among all those of Samā, Sūmra and other princes, continues well remembered and illustrious among Sindhians to the present day, is striking testimony to his exceptional excellence as a ruler. Among his virtues was that, so rare in the East, of recognising true worth in others, and giving his confidence where it was best deserved. His minister, Daryā Khān, served him well and wisely, and probably no small part of Jām Nanda's fame was due to this man's loyal and able administration. All Sindh from Bakhar, and beyond it, to the sea obeyed the greatest of the Samā princes, and as the Court at Delhi had enough to do in attending to matters that more nearly concerned it than the subordination of a distant province—to say nothing of the memories of what their contests with the Samās had cost the Tughlaq sovereigns—Jām Nanda enjoyed absolute independence. Nevertheless the shadow of coming calamity fell upon the Samās in his time. The Arghūns now began to threaten Sindh.

The great Arghūn chief Zū'n-Nūn Beg, who, towards the end of the fifteenth century, was appointed by Sultān Husayn Mīrzā of Herāt to the Governorship of Qandahār, finding the territory under his control insufficient to satisfy his needs and his ambition, proceeded to enlarge his borders in an easterly direction, and crossing the Amrān range, annexed Pishīng, Shāl (Quetta), and Mastūng. His sons, Shāh Beg and Muhammed Beg, next descended the Bolān Pass, and added Sīwī (or Sībī) to their father's possessions. But Sīwī was in Jām Nanda's territory, and that prince despatched a strong force under Daryā Khān, who seems now to have received the title of Mubārak Khān, to expel the intruders. Mubārak Khān came upon the Arghuns at Jalūgīr, a place in the Bolān Pass, near Bībī Nānī, inflicted a crushing defeat on them, and killed their leader, Muhammed Beg. This was the last display of real vigour by

[100] The "Beg Lār Nama" gives 914 H. as the date of Jām Nanda's death.

a Samā prince. It sufficed for the time, and the Arghūns, hardy and tried soldiers as they were, ventured no more into Sindh during Jām Nanda's reign.[101]

The defeat of the Arghūns at Jalūgīr took place about 1486.[102] In 1507 Mīr Zū'n-Nūn lost his life in the bloody field of Maruchak, when Shaybānī Khān invaded Khurāsān. His eldest son, Shāh Beg, soon found Qandahār a most difficult position to maintain, as Bābar, who had crossed the Hindū Kūsh and established himself in Qabul in 1504, now began to move southward and claimed the Qandahār territory as his own. Partly by force of arms, but more by adroit diplomacy, he managed to hold his own for some years, but Bābar gave him no peace. There was danger too from Shāh Ismā'īl, now in possession of Herāt. Thus placed between two adversaries, with neither of whom he could hope to contend successfully, Shāh Beg turned once more to Sindh. Jām Firūz had succeeded his father Jam Nanda at Ṭhaṭa, and was now, by his weakness of character, indolence and vices undoing all the good work of the previous reign. Disorder and discontent were rife throughout Sindh, and many of the chiefs were ready to accept a new ruler. Everything favoured Shāh Beg, who retook Sīwī and gained possession of Fathpur close to Gandāva. For a time he was greatly distressed by the smallness of his resources, for his new acquisitions brought him little revenue; but the richer country to the south lay open to an active and adventurous raider. He made a rush upon Chānduka and onwards to *Bāghbān* and *Gāhā*,[103] near Sēwan, highly fertile and flourishing

[101] So says Mīr M'aṣūm; but other writers, such as Abu'l-Fazal, Nizāmū'd-Dīn and Ferishta, referred to by Erskine in his history of the two first Tīmūri sovereigns (I. 343 n.), assert that the Arghūns promptly avenged the death of Muhammed Beg, and even at this time captured Bakhar and Sēwan. But Mīr M'aṣūm is a far more reliable authority for this period, both because he was born and bred at Bakhar, and had means of ascertaining from his father, who died in 1583, as well as from his grandfather, accurate information on the local events of the early part of the century; and also because it is evident from his history that he had no bias against either Samās or Arghūns, though perhaps his sympathies were rather with the latter.

[102] Erskine says Sīwī was taken in 1485. The affair in the Bolān Pass would probably take place the next year.

[103] Bāghbān is a township 27 miles north of Sēwan; Gāhā another, 21 miles north-west of that place. In English writings Gāhā appears as *Kahan*, because the Persian of Mīr M'aṣūm has کاهان, the distinctive dash of the *Gāf* being, as usual, omitted in manuscript, and a final *nūn* added for phonetic purposes, as in Sindh a final long vowel is usually nasalised in pronunciation. Sir H. Elliot took this place to be *Kāhan* in the Marri country, celebrated for its defence by a detachment of the 5th Bombay Regiment in 1840. Both Bāghbān and Gāhā are mentioned in the A-in-i-Akbarī as *Mahals*, or subdivisions, of the Sarkār of Sīwastān.

tracts, whence he gathered a rich booty. Thus supplied with some means of subsidising troops he soon afterwards collected a force strong enough to enable him to enter on a serious invasion of Sindh and advance against Ṭhaṭa itself. At the end of 1519 he marched southward by Sēwan and the Laki hills, meeting with no opposition, and soon arrived in the neighbourhood of Ṭhaṭa. Here he was stopped by an obstacle which, if properly turned to account by the Sindhians, might have kept him out of the capital, and perhaps have changed the issue of the campaign. This was the Kalrī. "In those days" (says Mir M'aṣūm) "the bulk of the river flowed (through the channel) to the north of Ṭhaṭa; consequently Shah Beg waited there some days considering how he was to cross this river (*daryā*); when it happened that a courier, who had crossed by a ford, arrived on the ground where he was. Some men on guard seized and threatened the man, whereupon he showed them the ford."

It is satisfactory to get such distinct information as to the course of the river at a given point and at a known date. In 1519, the Kalrī, we find was the principal channel of the Indus. It is curious that Mir M'aṣūm calls it the *Khānwāh.* This may be a mistake for *Khānāh,* a name by which the lower part of the Kalrī is called; but if there was no mistake the name Khānwāh indicates that there had been some artificial work carried out in connection with the Kalrī (the ancient Sindhu-Sāgara), to which the title of the person under whose direction the work was done had, according to common custom, been attached. It would have been no difficult matter by a certain amount of excavation at the head of the Kalrī, or even by making a new head to it, to turn a strong current from the main river into the old channel; and that once effected, the stream would soon cut a broader way for itself till the bulk of its water took the new direction. Such a work may have been executed in consequence of the volume of the Kalrī having begun to diminish, and with a view to maintain sufficient means of irrigation in the northern parts of the Sākro district—a matter of high importance to the capital now become so populous. It may even have been carried out as a defensive measure—to afford greater security to Ṭhaṭa in view of the aggressive proceedings of the Arg͟hūns. In either case it would be just such a work as the able and energetic minister, Daryā Khan, would be likely to inaugurate, and from him the whole channel may have acquired a new name.[104]

Crossing the Kalrī, or Khānwāh, without opposition, Shāh Beg traversed the few miles of country intervening between the stream and Ṭhaṭa, and found the Samā forces drawn up to meet him outside the city. Jām Firūz took care to remain within the walls, but the fine old Minister, Daryā Khān, took command. It was the last service he was to render to his country and his worthless sovereign. The Samās fought long and well, but were overmatched by the hardy Arghūns. Daryā Khān was taken prisoner and, with many other Samās, was at once put to death. Jām Firūz of course "set his face towards flight," and "crossing the river," that is to say, the Baghār, hurried to *Pir Ār*, 13 miles south of Ṭhaṭa.[105] The battle of Ṭhaṭa, which was fought on the 11th Muḥarram 926 (2nd January, 1520), gave Shāh Beg possession of Sindh; but he had doubts as to his present ability to hold the entire country. When, therefore, Jām Firūz had made his submission in the abject manner thought appropriate to a thoroughly crushed opponent, Shāh Beg restored to him the portion of his former territories lying south of the latitude of the Lakī Pass, and kept North Sindh for himself. He now reduced Sēwan, which had closed its gates against him, and Ṭalṭī. The latter place, we find, was then on the left bank of the river, as Shāh Beg's troops had to be carried across in boats to the attack.[106] Meanwhile a Samā chief, named Salāhu'd-Dīn, who, on Jām Nanda's death, had disputed, and for a time successfully, the succession to the throne, but had eventually been compelled to leave Sindh and fly to Guzerat, again appeared in the Delta country to try conclusions with Jām Firūz. The latter now applied for succour to his late conqueror and new ally, who promptly summoned his son, Shāh Husayn, from Shāl, whither he had just returned after two years' absence at the

[104] It seems certain that a natural, and very ancient, channel would not have received such a name as a matter of mere fancy or caprice, and irrespective of any occurrence connecting it in a special manner with the act of some well-known personage. There is another *Khānwāh*, leading from the Kalrī, which must not be confounded with the latter. Whether it is to this or to the larger channel that the Tarīkh-i-Tāhirī refers when it says that "the Khānwāh was made by Daryā Khān to irrigate the Sākro Pargana and other lands along the base of the hills, and those surrounding Ṭhaṭa," I am not aware.

[105] Thus it is seen that at a time of the year when the Indus is at its lowest both the branches surrounding Ṭhaṭa were flowing in 1520.

[106] A large part of the old channel of the river still exists to the south of Ṭalṭī, and contains a fine sheet of water known as the *Ṭalṭī-Dhandh*.

Court of Bābar in Qābul, and sent him to Thaṭa with a body of Arghūn troops. With these and a contingent under Jām Firūz, Shāh Husayn advanced against Salāhu'd-Dīn who had fallen back on the Jūn district, and coming upon him there, utterly routed his army. Salāhu'd-Dīn, and a son of his, lost their lives in the action, and their followers who escaped fled to Guzerat. In Northern Sindh chiefs and people speedily submitted to the vigorous Arghūn who, though savage and ruthless when resisted, was disposed to be conciliatory towards his new subjects. Shāh Beg took up his quarters at Sakhar and at once applied himself to the work of repressing local disorder, as well as to the restoration and enlargement of the fortifications of the island fort of Bakhar, for which purpose he utilised the materials existing at the long-ruined capital Alor, 5 miles to the east of Bakhar.

But during his conquest of Sindh Shāh Beg had formed the project of a much greater enterprise. This was the invasion of Guzerat, then under the rule of Sultān Bahādur. On Sindh he seemed to set no great value in comparison with the richer prize lying farther eastward, and he even promised to restore his former possessions to Jām Firūz in return for that prince's aid in the conquest of Guzerat. In December 1521 he started from Bakhar with a large force towards Lower Sindh, but in the Chānduka district a favourite officer, Mīr Fāzil Kokaltāsh, fell sick and had to return to Sakhar, where he soon died. In the loss of his old friend Shāh Beg saw an evil omen for himself, and conceived a presentiment of his own approaching end. However, after the funeral ceremonies at Sakhar, he resumed his march and reached the district of *Agham* in Lower Sindh.[107] From his camp here he sent to summon Jam Firūz to attend and accompany him to Guzerat. But now he sickened. On his march he had received the news of Bābar's successes in the Panjāb which led him to predict that the sovereign who had deprived him of his Qandahār territory would eventually deprive him of Sindh also. The depression which this reflection caused aggravated his illness and he died at Agham, apparently after a long stay there, on the 22nd Sh'abān, 928 H., or 16th July 1522 A.D.[108]

[107] Some 30 miles south-east of Haydarābād.

[108] In the chronology of all this period I follow Mīr M'aṣūm as one who is certainly likely to have been the best informed, as his father must have known Shāh Beg and was not likely to have made a mistake about the date of his death. This date too Mīr M. confirms by a chronogram, namely, *Shahr Sh'abān* (month Sha'bān) = 928.

The news of Shāh Beg's death was received by Jām Firūz in Ṭhaṭa with a delight which, under all the circumstances, was perhaps excusable; but, with his usual fatuity, he allowed himself to manifest his feelings in the most public manner by ordering the drums to be beaten. He thus gave Shāh Ḫusayn, the son and successor of Shah Beg, an excuse which, in spite of his indignation at the outrage, was probably not altogether unwelcome, for putting an end to Samā rule and bringing all Sindh under his own authority. This policy would the more readily suggest itself to him that he must now have recognised all the risks involved in the Guzerat project which, if successful—a matter very far from certain—would eventually bring him into collision with Bābar, the man whom he had such good cause to respect and fear, who was at this time carrying all before him in Northern India. Accordingly, on the completion of the funeral ceremonies, Shah Ḫusayn marched on Ṭhaṭa. Jam Firūz fled to Kachchh, and now, strangely enough, for the first time in his life began to display some energy. Collecting a considerable body of troops in the province where, as a Samā prince, he must have found abundant sympathy, he returned to Sindh. But, matched against such a man as Shāh Ḫusayn, he had small chance of restoring his fortunes. The Samās and Arghūns met for a final trial of strength in *Chāchkān*, a district in the Eastern Delta country, where a hard-fought battle ended in complete victory for Shāh Ḫusayn. Jām Firūz escaped to Guzerat, where he found an asylum with his connection by marriage, Sultan Bahādur, and never saw Sindh again. And thus ended Samā rule. Following Mīr M'aṣūm's chronology, this battle must have been fought in 1523, so that the entire period of the Samā dominion was just 190 years.[109]

Writers who lived in Eastern India, and far from the scene of these events, make the date of Shāh Beg's death 930 H., and Erskine, in his History (I. 376), follows them, though he is disposed to accept Mīr M.'s chronology generally. The fact is the chronology of the Arghūn invasions of Sindh, of Bābar's dealings with the Arghūns, and of his invasions of India, is involved in confusion and obscurity. Where, therefore, a date is given, and supported by a chronogram, by one possessing peculiar means of learning the truth, I think it ought not to be set aside unless on the clearest evidence of its incorrectness.

[109] The actual site of the battlefield is not named by Mīr M., but I think it is perhaps to be discovered in one of the curious so-called predictions attributed to the mysterious people who are known in Sindh as the *Māmū-ī-Fakīrs*, and are said to have lived in the earlier times of the Samā princes. Burton (Sindh, p. 89) gives the prediction in the following form :

Shāh Ḫusayn was now master of all Sindh, but he had the prudence to acknowledge the overlordship of Bābar even before the latter had won his way to Delhi. The second Arghūn prince had inherited the political ability as well as the manly and vigorous character of his father and grandfather; also, it must be added, the fierce and cruel temper of his race. The project of invading Guzerat being abandoned, he gave his attention to the establishing of order in Sindh and to the extension of his territory northwards. He overran all the country on the left bank of the Indus up to the Panjnad, and at a later period, under instructions from Bābar, he took Multān and handed it over to the Emperor. With him Shāh Ḫusayn was always careful to maintain the most friendly and loyal relations. His two years' experience at Qabul had inspired him with a genuine respect for Bābar, and at the same time, perhaps, had led him to form an unfavourable opinion of Bābar's eldest son and heir. At all events, Hūmayūn had not been long on the throne when Shāh Ḫusayn began to ponder the question whether it was any longer politic to identify his fortunes with the cause of the Tīmūrides. About the time when Hūmayūn's troubles with Shēr Shāh were approaching an acute stage,

"Kāre Kābāre jhūro lagando chah pahar.
Mirmichī māre. Suku wasandī Sindhrī."

"At Kāro Kābāro a battle shall be fought lasting six watches (18 hours).
The Mirmichī shall be beaten. Sindh shall enjoy peace."

I have slightly altered his translation to make it more exact. He says that Sindhīs explain this prediction as referring to Sir C. Napier's victory at *Daba*, and the extinction of the rule of the Tālpur Mīrs; but that "Kāro Kābāro" cannot be accounted for, no action ever having been fought at such a place. He accepts the popular interpretation of the prophecy, and agrees with the popular opinion that the inexplicable term *Mirmichī* designates the Tālpur chiefs. It is certainly true that the popular views on these points are as he describes them, but I believe them to be totally mistaken. *Kāro Kābāro* is not an imaginary name. The place intended is evidently *Khārī Khabarlo*, a township in the present Ṭanḍo Bāgo Pargana, *part of ancient Chāchkān;* and I think it extremely probable that this was the battlefield in which the pride of the Samās was quenched, and that the prediction (perhaps safely uttered by somebody after the event) refers to that fatal day. The Māmū-ī-Fakīrs, as the legend says, were put to death by the Samā, Jām Tamāchī. It was, indeed, after the execution that each severed head uttered in succession one of the well-known prophecies. What more likely than that some later admirer of men fully credited with divine inspiration should gratify his vengeful feelings and his fancy by inventing a Māmū-ī prediction in relation to a catastrophe which he regarded as the divine retribution for Jām Tamāchī's crime? And if we compare historical facts we shall find that they support my view much more than the popular one. The battle in Chāchkān is described by Mīr M'aṣūm (who very likely was acquainted with the Māmūī prophecies, but never on any occasion refers to them, and who was apparently ignorant of the precise situation of the battlefield) as "lasting from early morning till well on in the afternoon." He says that the Samās, according to the

Shāh Ḫusayn sent a confidential officer to Delhi to gain information as to the true position of affairs there. This officer's report was most unfavourable to Hūmāyun, whom he found exhibiting an indolence, apathy and addiction to pleasure that augured badly for the future of one exposed in a newly conquered country to the hostility of a powerful party headed by such an astute and vigorous character as Shēr Shāh. Shāh Ḫusayn at once decided to abandon all active allegiance to the Emperor, and for the present to assume a position of neutrality.

In the beginning of the year 1541, Hūmāyūn arrived at Rohrī. Defeated and a fugitive, he still commanded a body of troops which might form the nucleus of a new army wherewith to regain his throne. But some base for his future operations was indispensable, and this he hoped to find in Sindh. This, however, was what Shāh Husayn was determined not to let him have. He had no confidence in Hūmāyūn, whose unsteadiness of character allowed little hope of his retrieving his fortunes; and he was much too prudent to provoke a quarrel with the strong man at Delhi by showing any active sympathy with the cause of the fallen Emperor. In outward forms

Sindhian custom when it is resolved to die fighting, bound themselves together, using their turbans and other parts of their dress for the purpose, and that 20,000 fell in the fight—a gross exaggeration, no doubt, but it may be taken to indicate that the action was exceptionally hard fought and bloody. It would, therefore, be no very extreme use of poetical amplification to describe such a battle as lasting six watches. The battle of Daba, on the other hand, lasted but one *pahar*, and the field is sixty good miles from Khārī Khaḅarlo. It is therefore difficult to see how the prediction can refer to the case of the Tālpur Mirs. The word *Mirmichi*, which nobody in Sindh can explain, is evidently one that has died out of popular memory in the course of three and a half centuries. It was probably some depreciatory epithet, or nickname, applied by ill-wishers (for instance, perhaps by Sūmras) to Samā princes; and it must have been current at the time of the prediction, which otherwise would have been without meaning for any one. Nobody can produce a tittle of evidence to prove that the mysterious name was ever bestowed on the Tālpurs previous to their downfall; and it is certain that those chiefs never fought a battle at Khārī Khabarlo, or anywhere within many miles of it. How Jām Firūz came to fight there is easily explained. An army coming from Kaḏhchh would naturally take that direction; and, which is still a more obvious explanation, a commander who desired to have a handy line of retreat to Guzerat available in case of need would take up such a position; for Khārī Khaḅarlo is close to the old track from Chāchkān to Guzerat *viâ* Mitti, Islāmkoṭ and Pārkar. We are told, accordingly, that after the battle Jām Firūz fled to that country. The meaning of Khārī Khaḅarlo (properly—loī) is "place of salt land and *Khaḅar* bushes." Jām Firūz, I may add, lost his life in Guzerat. In 1535 he was a prisoner in Hūmāyūn's camp at Cambay, and he was killed by his guards to prevent his being rescued when a party of Bhils and Gowārs made a night attack on the camp. (Erskine, II., 62, n.)

of courtesy he was not wanting. He received Hūmāyūn's ambassadors with the utmost respect; he offered to make provision out of his revenues for the maintenance of the Emperor and his followers; but he evaded compliance with the summons to attend the Court at Rohrī, and he kept Bakhar and Sēwan̲, the strong places of the country which Hūmāyūn was particularly anxious to occupy, firmly closed against him. With the further course of events in Upper Sindh—Hūmāyūn's inactivity; the thwarting of his plans by his selfish and treacherous brothers, who soon deserted him; the dearth which threatened all with starvation, and at last compelled the Emperor to move; his visit to *Pāṭ*,[110] where, in the midst of all his troubles, he found time to fall in love with and to marry the lady Hamīda, who became the mother of Akbar; his attempt to capture Sēwan̲ by a sudden assault; his failure in this, and in the regular siege which followed; the wrecking of his army by disease and desertion; his headlong flight from Sēwan̲ back to Rohrī, pursued by Shāh Husayn's troops; his march thence into the deserts of Mārwār in hope of obtaining succour from Rao Māldēo; his failure in this object, and the narrow escape of himself and his followers from perishing of thirst in the wilds of Jesalmīr and Mallānī—this memoir is not concerned. The thread of the narrative may be picked up again at the arrival of Hūmāyūn and his followers, now greatly reduced in numbers and in sore distress, at the fort of Ūmarkoṭ in August 1542.

At Ūmarkoṭ, Hūmāyūn at last met with one who was not only sympathetic and hospitable, but also prepared to render him active and valuable assistance in his designs on Sindh. This was the Sodha chief, Rānā Parsād. The Rānā was at deadly feud with Shāh

[110] The ruins of the town of Pāṭ where, in August 1541, Hūmāyūn married Ḥamīda and where, sometime later (*circa* 1545), his brother Kāmrān married the daughter of Shāh Ḥusayn, lie a little to the east of the present village of that name in the Kakar Pargana, and bear the name *Pāṭ Kuhna* (Old Pāṭ). On the west side of the old site, and separating it from the new village, is an old channel, now containing standing water. In this channel, says a local chronicle relating to that part of the country, the river ran at the time of Hūmāyūn's visit, so that, coming from Babarlo (a little south of Rohrī) by Bhēlāṇī (in Kandhīārā) and Darbelo, he had no water to cross. The river now runs (or did a few years ago) 5 or 6 miles east, and also 3 miles south, of Pāṭ. The place gave its name to an extensive and very fertile tract of country in former times. In the Aīn-ī-Akbarī the *Mahal* of Pāṭ appears as the most productive of the entire Sarkār of Sīwastān. Old Pāṭ, lying in the route of Madad K̲h̲ān's invasion in 1798, was, like hundreds of other towns and villages so situated, laid in ruins by that desolating ruffian.

Ḫusayn, who had put his father to death; and, welcoming an opportunity for vengeance, he offered to make common cause with the Emperor, to place 2,000 horsemen of his own at his disposal, and to procure for him the assistance of 5,000 men of the Sindhī tribe of Samēja. The offer was gladly accepted, though but a few months later, Hūmāyūn's habitual apathy, and his inability to control his unruly followers, lost him an alliance which, prudently utilised, might have won Sindh for him. After considerable delay at Ūmarkoṭ, the Emperor placed his family in the fort, vacated for this purpose by the Rānā, and, following the latter's advice, proceeded towards *Jūn*, a central position in the Delta country, 75 miles south-west of Ūmarkoṭ, and 50 miles north-east of Ṭhaṭa. Four days later, on the 15th October, 1542, Ḫamīda Bānū Bēgam gave birth to Akbar in the fort of Ūmarkoṭ.[111]

Jūn, the chief town of a fertile and populous district, was situated on the left bank of the Rēn. Mir M'aṣūm says of it: "Jūn is situated on the bank of the river Sind (he ought to have said "on a branch of the river Sind"), and is eminent among the towns of Sind by reason of its numerous gardens and water-courses, and its exquisite fruits." It was just the place where Hūmāyūn, passionately fond of gardens, would delight to take up his quarters, and where he would idle away much precious time.[112] This is the first occasion of an historical reference to the Rēn, a name of which Mir M'aṣum seems to have been ignorant. This portion of his history, indeed, indicates a curious lack of knowledge of the geography of the Delta country. At that time (1542), and down to the middle of the eighteenth century, the Indus ran 3 to 4 miles east of Ṭanḍo Muhammed Khān; and 5 to 7 miles (the exact spot has not yet been discovered) south-east of that place it threw off the Rēn which, as mentioned in the first section, ran towards the eastern extremity of the Delta. Thus the point at which the Rēn left the main river constituted a true Delta head. Whether this branch stream was

[111] The Sindh Gazetteer says that Akbar marched through Ūmarkot in 1591 to conquer Sindh. This is imaginary history. Akbar was in Sindh as an infant in arms;—never later.

[112] Prince Dārā Shikoh spent a short time in Jūn when fleeing from his brother in 1658, and there his wife died. It was the chief of Jūn who, after entertaining him and feigning much cordiality, basely caused him to be seized and then handed him over to Aurangzīb. The ruins of Jūn are to be seen two miles south-east of the present Tando Ghulām Ḫaydar.

perennial or not is a question which we are without sufficient evidence to decide with certainty; but there are undoubtedly some grounds for an affirmative conclusion. When Shāh Ḫusayn learnt that Hūmāyūn had taken up his position at Jūn he established a camp of observation 5½ miles higher up the channel of the Rēn, but on its right bank. To this place he gave the name *Fath Bāgh*, probably in honour of the successes already obtained, and of others anticipated in his dealings with the Emperor. The object of selecting this position would be to close all communication *by water* between Hūmayūn's camp and the main river; to prevent the Emperor from getting possession of boats in any large number, and using these for the conveyance of men and material in an advance on Ṭhaṭa; to block, in short, the great highway to the capital. But this would not prove that the Rēn was flowing in the month of October when Hūmāyūn arrived at Jūn, and still less at the time (perhaps November) of Shāh Ḫusayn's taking post at Fath-Bāgh; for that post may have been occupied in the expectation that Hūmāyūn would stay long in Jūn (he did in fact spend nine months there), and to hinder access to the main river when, six months later, the periodical rise of the latter should take place, and, of course, fill the Rēn channel. Other incidents bearing on the question leave it in the same uncertainty. Thus we are told that Shāh Ḫusayn "pressed upon the imperial army . . . . both by land *and water*," but no indication is given of the particular period at which this pressure was exerted, and it would rather seem to have occurred in the latter part of Hūmāyūn's stay at Jūn when of course the Rēn was flowing. Again, Hūmāyūn sent a foraging party into the "Pargana of Baṭhoro," *west* of the Rēn.[113] This party was overtaken, and almost totally destroyed, by a detachment of Shāh Ḫusayn's troops. At night the people in the camp at Jūn heard some one calling from the right bank of the Rēn *for a boat to ferry him over*. A boat was sent, and the caller proved to be the second in command of the ill-fated party. But the disaster in Baṭhoro is shown to have occurred not long before Hūmāyūn vacated Jūn, which we know he did on the 10th July, and therefore it must be dated not earlier than June; though even if it happened in May it would not prove that the Rēn was a perennial stream, as in that

[113] Erskine says (II. 260) it was sent to a place *in the Tharī*, meaning, presumably, in the Thar districts, far *east* of the Rēn. Mīr M'aṣūm, here certainly right, says "Pargana Bathoro."

month it would in any case be flowing in consequence of the periodical inundation. In favour of the view that the stream was perennial are the facts that a very large part of the Eastern Delta country was dependent on it for irrigation; and that so long as the Rēn carried water that tract of country was noted for its fertility and flourishing condition. It was called *Chāchkān*, "from the village and tribe of *Chāchak*," says the Tuḥfatu'l-Kirām. When Hūmāyūn first arrived in Sindh Shāh Ḫusayn pointed out to him in a letter that Chāchkān would be much more suitable for his residence than the Bakhar country, and described the former as "celebrated for its populousness and abundance of corn." This would hardly have been the case if the Rēn had been a mere inundation channel. On the whole the balance of probability seems to be on the side of the opinion that the stream was either perennial or that it flowed for at all events eight or nine months of the year.

Hūmāyūn spent nine months in Jūn closely watched and constantly harassed by Shāh Ḫusayn. The opportunity of a brilliant success likely to be gained by a bold attack on Shāh Ḫusayn while the assistance of Rānā Parsād was available was allowed to pass away, and while the emperor lingered indolently in his intrenchments his disorderly followers did what was in their power to ruin his cause by giving vent to their personal jealousies and even by deserting to the enemy. Nor were Musulmān intolerance and haughtiness to be debarred from the pleasure of openly showing scorn of Hindūs, even at the risk of alienating an ally whose co-operation was essential to the success of the imperial plans. One of Hūmāyūn's officers grossly insulted Rānā Parsād, who forthwith abandoned the Emperor and retired to Ūmarkoṭ in disgust, a step immediately followed by the defection of the Sindhian tribe which the Rānā had induced to side against Shāh Ḫusayn. The annihilation of the detachment in Baṭhoro was due to jealousy between the leaders, and to the inaction of Tardī Beg who, always distinguished for gallantry, was now moved by some feeling of pique, or by sheer bad temper, to refuse efficient support. At this crisis of his calamities it was Hūmāyūn's good fortune to be joined by an old and loyal counsellor in the person of Bīram Khān. This man opened negotiations with Shāh Ḫusayn with the object of concluding peace, and obtaining for the Emperor a safe passage through Sindh to Shāl and Qandahār. Shāh Ḫusayn, prudently anxious to avoid a decisive action with one whom he knew to be resolute and dangerous when driven to extremity, eagerly closed with proposals which, without further risk, would rid Sindh of Hūmāyūn's exceedingly troublesome presence. He engaged to furnish the Emperor with money, grain and transport, and proceeded to throw a temporary bridge across the Rēn at Jūn.[114] Over this the Emperor and his troops passed on the 10th July 1543. The main channel of the Indus remained to be passed, and the point selected for the crossing was 12 or 13 miles north-west of Jūn, where now all is dry, the river running 16 miles to the west, and its course in Hūmāyūn's time traceable only by means of half-obliterated hollows. I have been able to fix the point of crossing by the aid of two indications supplied by histories which relate these events. Both Jauhar and Gulbadan Bēgam, when giving an account of the passage of the Indus, state that the emperor reached the right bank at the village of *Ronāī*,[115] where Shāh Ḫusayn had the promised supplies waiting for him. There is no such village now, but there *is* a township in the Gūnī Pargana, called *Roshanāī*, situated on the *right* bank of an old river channel, and it contains the ruins of a village which there can be little doubt are those of Gulbadan Bēgam's Ronāī. In the course of copying the middle syllable of the name has dropped out in the Memoirs, or it may be that the good lady herself made some mistake. That there is no mistake about the identification can be shown by other evidence. In one of the local chronicles—either the "Tārīkh-i-Tāhirī," or the "Beg-Lār-Nāma"—the author, decidedly unfavourable to the Arghūns, when describing the death of Shāh Ḫusayn, remarks that it occurred *close to the place where the Sindhian prince had made the emperor cross the river;* and he evidently regards the fact of the death occurring here as a judgment on Shāh Ḫusayn. Now, the Arghūn prince died at the village of *'Aārīpoṭā* (sometimes, but incorrectly, written *'Alīpotra* in the histories), which still exists, and is 1¾ miles from the ruined site in Roshanāī. 'Aārīpoṭa also was on the river: in fact Shāh Ḫusayn died on board a boat, and not actually in the place itself. It is evident, then, that the place where the Emperor crossed the Indus on his way to Qandahār is now ascertained with certainty.

[114] That it was possible for him to bridge the Rēn at a time when the inundation must have nearly reached its maximum height is proof that the channel was neither very broad nor the current very strong.

[115] So far as my memory serves me (for I write under the disadvantage of being unable to consult these works again), Gulbadan Bēgam gives the name Ronāī, and Jauhar another somewhat like Ronāī.

The fact is interesting both from the historical event connected with the site, and also from our being thus enabled to fix with accuracy the course of the main river in this part of the country in 1543.[116]

Here we part company with Hūmāyūn who passed by Sēwan̲ to the north-west frontier and returned to Sindh no more. Shāh H̲usayn continued to rule in Sindh in virtual independence till 1555. Towards the end of his life he became palsied, fell into intemperate habits and suffered all the good effects of his previous strong government to be undone by low and worthless favourites. His death occurred on the 5th February 1555, his reign having lasted 33 years; and with him closed the Argh̲ūn line which numbered but two princes.

Shāh H̲usayn left no heir, the only son ever born to him having died in infancy. He had given his daughter in marriage to Prince Kāmrān, in the expectation that the latter would succeed him in Sindh; but the hope of establishing the succession in the princely line of Tīmūr vanished when Kāmrān was blinded. The cruel deed, however, which incapacitated Kāmrān from reigning was certainly for the good of Sindh, as the prince never would have contented himself with a territory coming so short of what he considered himself entitled to; and the country would have been kept in constant turmoil while its new sovereign was using it as a mere stepping-stone to wider dominion. Not, indeed, that Sindh fared much better as the case was. Under Shāh H̲usayn the country had been divided into two subordinate governments. North Sindh, from Bakhar to Sēwan̲, was administered by Sultān Mahmūd, son of Shāh Beg's favourite, Mīr Fāzil Kokaltāsh; Southern Sindh was kept in the hands of the prince himself, but, after him, the most influential person in the lower province was Mīrzā 'Īsà, head of the Tarkhāns who had accompanied Shāh Beg when he invaded the country. Shortly before Shāh H̲usayn's death these two men secretly agreed to await that event in loyalty, and then to divide Sindh between them; *Lakī* being made, as in the case of Shāh Beg and Jām Firūz, the point of division

[116] Roshanāī is not marked in the maps of the Topographical Survey. It was, in fact, only a *Makān*, or subdivision of a township, until a few years ago when, during the revision of the Settlement Survey in Gūnī, it was constituted a *Dēh* or township. This case furnishes another instance of the aid to be obtained from township names in tracing old sites when the actual town or village has disappeared, and its name has been forgotten. Roshanāī is situated six miles nearly due south of Ṭanḍo Muhammed K̲h̲ān, and close to the road (on the east side) leading from that place into the southern districts.

between the two territories. This compact seems to have been entered into by Mīrzā 'Īsà to suit the convenience of the moment, and with the intention of eventually constituting himself heir to all Shāh Ḫusayn's dominion. But in Sulṭān Mahmūd he had an opponent of no mean capacity, and noted from his boyhood for personal bravery and resolution. Sulṭān Mahmūd could not, indeed, gain possession of Sēwan̲, to which he was entitled under the secret agreement; for there the local officers took advantage of an unsettled succession to set up for themselves; and, with the Tarkhān chief already in the field against him, he was not in a position to do more than hold the country to the north of Sīwastān. This, however, he prepared to do with his accustomed energy.

On the other side Mīrzā 'Īsà showed equal determination to carry out his object of acquiring supremacy in Sindh. Probably far stronger in numbers than Sultān Mahmūd, he soon disposed of the pretensions of the Sīwastān chiefs, and was able to gain that coveted territory permanently for Lower Sindh. His next move was the invasion of Sulṭān Mahmūd's country on the left bank of the river, and here he advanced as far north as to Bakhar itself, where he fought two engagements, apparently without any very decisive result. But now occurred an event which compelled him to retreat in hot haste to Ṭhaṭa, and which formed a remarkable episode in the history of the relations of Sindh with foreign countries.

VII.

THE PORTUGUESE IN THE DELTA.

On Shāh Ḫusayn's death, Mīrzā 'Īsà, desiring to close all controversy with Sulṭān Mahmūd in the speediest and most effectual manner by bringing irresistible force to bear against him, and finding his own means of coercion inadequate to that end, bethought him of the foreigners whose prowess on the western coast of India was now gaining for them in the East the highest reputation as a fighting people. With their assistance North Sindh might easily be won from Sultān Mahmūd, and reunited to the Ṭhaṭa province. The Mīrza accordingly despatched an embassy to Bassein, the seat of government of the northern Portuguese province, to ask for the aid of a military force, all the charges of which he would defray, and to offer in return special commercial privileges which it was of course known would be a strong inducement to the foreigners to comply with the Mīrzā's request. The local histories pass lightly over this important episode in the history of Lower Sindh; Mīr M'aṣūm bestowing only a sentence or two on it, and the "Tārīkh-i-Tāhirī," which gives the fullest account of it, representing it as far less serious than it really was. The following narrative, taken from "The History of the Discovery and Conquest of India by the Portuguese," a translation, by Capt. John Stevens, of the Spanish work of Manuel de Faria y Souza (London, 1695), no doubt sets matters in a much truer light. "Antonio Barreto . . . . returned to Bazaim where he found the Governor receiving an embassy from the King of Cinde, who desired succour against a tyrant that infested him. We were desirous of this Prince's friendship, and thought fit to purchase it by relieving him. Seven hundred men were sent to him in 28 vessels, all commanded by Pedro Barreto Rolim. The fleet arrived safe at Tatá, the Court of the King of Cinde. The Prince who was there[117] visited Barreto, and sent word of his arrival to his father who was absent in the field. He answered desiring our Commander to wait till he advised what was fit to be done. Barreto stayed, and soon after, hearing the King was agreed with his enemy without giving him notice, he asked of the Prince leave to depart, and that he would pay the charge of the fleet as was promised by the Ambassador (to the Governor of Bassein). The answer was so little to satisfaction that Barreto landed his men, entered the city, and in the fury killed above 8000 persons, and destroyed by fire the value of above two millions of gold, after loading the vessels with one of the richest booties that had been taken in Asia. He lost not one man in this action. He spent eight days in destroying all on both sides Indus (that is between Ṭhaṭa and the coast). The fort of Bandel[118] made

[117] This was Mīrzā Jān Bābā, youngest son of Mīrzā 'Īsà, who was in charge of Ṭhaṭa during his father's absence in North Sindh. Several years after these events he was treacherously seized and put to death by his insane and savage eldest brother, Muhammed Bāqī.

[118] Lāharī Bandar is evidently the place intended. Bandel is perhaps a mistake for Bandar. In the next extract we shall see the place called *Baradel*. Both names might be corruptions of *Bārī-Dēwal*, "Dēwal estuary," but I have not met this name in local histories.

some resistance, but being taken was demolished. Gaspar de Monterroyo, a soldier of note, going accidentally into a wood, met some Blacks who bid him go no farther, for hard-by there was a serpent had just then devoured a bullock. He, desiring to see such a monster as they described, went on till he discovered the head, which was of a wonderful bigness, and, not satisfied, came so near as to touch it with his sword, and the monster lifted up its head, and he gave it such a fortunate stroke on a soft place that it soon after died. It was thirty foot long and proportionable in bigness.[119] Barreto returned thus victorious over men and monsters to Chaul" (II. 184, 185).

The narrative of the sack of Ṭhaṭa in the year 1555, contained in the extract above given, is by one whose sympathies were all on the side of the Portuguese chiefs and their masterful methods in India. Another writer, a French Jesuit, tells the same story from a point of view less favourable to the Portuguese, and adds an important piece of information which Faria y Souza had preferred to omit—namely, the final result to the Portuguese of their enterprise in Sindh. I translate from the work entitled, "Histoire des Découvertes et Conquêtes des Portugais dans le Nouveau Monde," par le Père Joseph François Lafitau, de la Compagnie de Jésus. Paris, 1733: "While the Gov.-General was at Bassein, he was visited by Ambassadors of the King of Cinde, called by a corruption of the name, King of Dulcinde. The Prince, whose country was near Diu,[120] desired assistance against a powerful neighbour, and promised to pay the expenses of the war, as well as to concede important advantages to the Portuguese in the matter of trade in his country. The Governor despatched to him Pierre Barretto Rolin, with a fleet of twenty-eight vessels[121] containing a land force of 700 men. But meanwhile the Prince, having come to terms with his enemy, only tried to beguile Pierre Barretto and would hear nothing more on the subject of his engagement to pay expenses. For a time Barretto dissembled his feelings in spite of the insolence of his

[119] The rock snake, the only representative (I think) of the Python family in Sindh, is found in the neighbouring Kohistān; not, so far as I know, in the Delta; and nowhere is this snake capable of swallowing a bullock. The monster described in the text would be a true Python, and an exceptionally large one.

[120] The good Father had perhaps got confused between Diu and Diul.

[121] These were large pinnaces, called in Portuguese *Fusta*. Faria y Souza gives the name of the commander of each vessel in this expedition.

followers, who openly reproached him with cowardice; but at last, after he had quietly laid in provisions for the return voyage, he found himself obliged to attack. He first took a mosque, and then the town of Ṭhaṭa, which his people sacked with inconceivable fury, not sparing even the dumb animals. It is said that nearly eight thousand souls perished at the cost to the Portuguese of only a few wounded men. The wealth consumed by fire is positively asserted to have exceeded two millions of gold, to say nothing of the booty taken, which was immense. After this they made similar expeditions on both banks of the river as they retired, leaving everywhere frightful traces of their passage and their fury. The retirement proved difficult, but, thanks to the good leading of the Commander, it was accomplished successfully; not a single tribe being left unharried as far as the fort of Baradel, at the entrance to the river, which they took by escalade and treated as they had done every other place. A violent storm avenged the many slain and the vast amount of pillage. Barretto was obliged to throw overboard all the spoils of so many ravaged places, and had the utmost difficulty in regaining Chaul" (II. pp. 536, 537). This second account is certainly incorrect in representing Mīrza 'Īsà as present in Thata when the Portuguese arrived there; and Faria y Souza's narrative is proved to be accurate in its statement on this point, because it is in agreement with the local histories which tell us that the Mīrzā was near Bakhar at the time, and that his son Jān Bābā was at Ṭhaṭa. Mīrzā 'Īsà, indeed, never saw the Portuguese at all, a fact which tells against the latter. Had Barreto waited a reasonable time all might have been settled according to agreement; for there is nothing to show that Mīrza 'Īsà was endeavouring to repudiate the engagements entered into by his ambassadors at Bassein; and it was out of all reason to expect that the young Mīrzā should satisfy important claims offhand and without authority from his father. The statement, moreover, that Mīrzā 'Īsà had concluded peace with his opponent before the Portuguese arrived seems to be contrary to the fact. The local histories are agreed in asserting that it was the news of the sack of Ṭhaṭa which induced the Mīrzā to abandon the campaign in North Sindh, where for the moment the balance of success was on his side. These histories may be accepted as absolutely trustworthy in the present question, because their authors were evidently in total ignorance of the reasons assigned by the Portuguese for their violent proceedings in the Delta, and never once allude to any differences between Mīrzā 'Īsà and his European allies. They in fact, for some reason or other, treat the devastating raid in the Delta as of such slight importance, and pass over it so quickly, that but for the reports of the Portuguese themselves, the event in its real proportions never would have been made known to later times. The truth probably is that the Mīrzā was not prepared for so prompt a response to the overtures which he made to the Portuguese; otherwise, well aware, as he must have been, of the daring character and piratical tendencies of those people, he would hardly have left his flourishing capital *totally unfortified and unguarded,*[122] to tempt their cupidity, while he himself and all his available forces were engaged in operations at a distance of nearly 300 miles from Ṭhaṭa. The Tarkhān Nāma no doubt gives the true explanation of the whole case when it says in a few simple words: "Intelligence arrived (at Bakhar) that the Firingīs, who were coming from Lāhorī Bandar to the assistance of Mīrzā 'Īsà Tarkhān, *finding the city of Ṭhaṭa unprotected*, had plundered it, set fire to it, and made the inhabitants prisoners" (Elliot, I. 324). The final judgment on the question must be that the excuses brought forward by the Portuguese for their sacking of Ṭhaṭa and subsequent raid in the Western Delta have no ground of fact to rest upon, and that those ruthless and murderous deeds were the outcome of mere greed and ferocity finding their opportunity in the temporary helplessness of the Delta people.

The remainder of Mīrzā Īsà's life was spent in hostilities, more or less acute, with Sultān Mahmūd, but, opposed by that resolute chief, he was never able to succeed in his cherished design of reuniting Sindh under the rule of a Tarkhān prince. His death occurred at the end of 1565, or the beginning of 1566, his reign having lasted between 10 and 11 years. His eldest son and successor, Muhammed Bāqī, seems to have been insane. After ruling for five years, in the course of which he put his brother Mīrzā Jān Bābā to death, starved to death his step-mother, and committed many other atrocities, he destroyed himself in 1571. His only

[122] This fact is not only asserted by the local historians, but made clear by the statement of the Portuguese themselves that they had not one man killed in the sacking of Ṭhaṭa.

surviving son, Mīrzā Pāyanda Muhammed,[123] being also insane, the latter's son, Mīrzā Jānī Beg, succeeded at Ṭhaṭa.

In 1574 Sulṭān Mahmūd died leaving no heir, and the Emperor Akbar sent an officer of his own to take charge of Bakhar and North Sindh, thus initiating the policy of bringing the entire province more directly under imperial control.

VIII.

THE CAMPAIGN OF THE IMPERIAL FORCES IN LOWER SINDH IN 1591–92.

THE position of successive chiefs in Sindh, fluctuating as it did between virtual independence and acknowledged subjection, according as a weak or a strong sovereign filled the imperial throne, or as calmness or trouble prevailed in the more central provinces, was a dangerous one for the ambitious characters among them. Mīrzā Jānī Beg was from the first strongly disposed to repudiate vassalage to the empire, and some seventeen years after his accession he was actually in arms against the imperial governor at Bakhar. On that occasion a timely submission to Akbar, ever clement and generous to those who threw themselves on his mercy, saved him from the consequences of rebellion. But the profession of obedience and loyalty forced on him by the exigencies of the moment was soon forgotten under the influence of the passion for independence, or for at least preserving the semblance of it. When Akbar had for some years made Lāhor his principal residence, and had there received the acknowledgments of their fealty by his other great vassals in the customary form of occasional attendance at his court, Jānī Beg kept himself aloof, thereby making a distinct demonstration of disrespect and disloyalty. The Emperor had now had enough of the pretensions of the Ṭhaṭa chiefs, and he proceeded to put an end once for all to the insolence and the power of Jānī Beg.

[123] Mīrzā Ṣalih Muhammed, the second and favourite son of Mīrzā 'Īsà, and one of the best of the Tarkhān chiefs, was assassinated in 1562 by a Baloch in revenge for the death of several of his family who had been executed by order of Ṣāliḥ Muhammed for their lawless conduct.

Mīrzā ʻAbdur'r-Rahīm, the Khān Khānān, and principal military officer of the empire, was despatched in the beginning of 1591 in command of a large force to Bakhar. There he spent the following hot season, and in September moved against Sēwan, the northern stronghold of the Tarkhāns, to which he laid siege. Meanwhile Jānī Beg had taken the field and encamped at Naṣrpūr on the left bank of the river, about 75 miles south-east of Sēwan.

The campaign is now interesting mainly because of its connection with a course of the Indus long since abandoned, and much of it difficult or impossible to trace at the present day with any certainty. In 1591 the river ran close to Sēwan,[124] but after passing that place some 8 or 10 miles its course lay much to the eastward of the present one. It ran probably very near Sakarand (whether at this period east or west of it is doubtful), and thence pursued the same south-easterly direction to Naṣrpūr, which place is 14 miles to the east of the present course of the Indus. Between Sakarand and Naṣrpūr the channel was known as the *Sāngra*, a name which European writers have sometimes transformed into *Sānkra* and *Sankrā*, and have confounded with *Sākra* which belongs to a Pargana of the Western Delta.[125] Jānī Beg's first intention was to make his stand at Naṣrpūr, but finding this place unsuitable for defence, he moved 10 miles higher up the left bank to a village called *Būhirī* or *Bohirī*, which, by copyist's errors, appears in the texts of some of the local histories as *Rohirī* and *Lohirī*. Near this he found an admirably defensive position in a large loop of land, formed by an abrupt recurving of the river, the neck of which he closed with strong earthworks armed with artillery. All other parts of the position were sufficiently protected, either by the river or by sandbanks so soft that, as the Tarkhān Nāma describes them, "if any one set foot on them he would sink up to his neck." The spot thus chosen for the entrenched camp was not only easily defensible, but offered the great advantage to Jānī Beg of a secure mooring-place for his

[124] This is to be gathered indirectly from references to Sēwan in the local histories, and directly from an observation of Mīr M'aṣūm's reporting the advice of his officers to the Khān Khānān ; "as Sēwan is on the line of road (from north to south) and is the *crossing-place* for our men and boats, it is best to take it first, &c."

[125] The name has been continued to the present day by its being applied to an inundation canal which runs through part of the course of the old Sāngra river channel. The Sangra is mentioned in Nādir Shāh's treaty of 1739 with the Emperor Muhammed Shah, in which the name appears to apply to a much greater length of the stream than was in accordance with usage in Sindh itself.

enormous fleet of boats. On land he was not strong enough to cope with the imperial forces; but the river he could command, and thus keep open his communications with all Lower Sindh and draw upon practically inexhaustible supplies. The case was very different with the imperialists, though for them matters were probably made worse than they need have been by their own mismanagement.

When Mīrzā Abdu'r-Rahīm learnt that Jānī Beg had advanced so far northwards as Nasrpūr he raised the siege of Sēwan, recrossed the river and marched along the left bank to meet the army of Lower Sindh.[126] Accompanying him was a war flotilla of twenty-five vessels.[127] On arriving at a point probably about 3 miles east or north-east of the present well-known village of *Bhiṭ Shāh,* he learnt that Jānī Beg's fleet was coming up the river to attack him; he accordingly moved close up to the bank at a point where a large sandbank caused the river to run in a comparatively narrow channel close under his position. Here he hastily lined the bank with earthworks to protect his guns, and awaited the attack, his flotilla probably moored at some little distance higher up the river.

Jānī Beg's fleet was commanded by the best of his officers, Khusrau Khān Charkas. He had arranged that a combined attack by the fleet and land forces should be made on the imperialists at an early hour in the morning, and with this object he himself started at nightfall with a squadron composed, according to the Ṭabaqāt-i-Akbarī (no doubt again exaggerating), of "more than a hundred *ghurābs* (or fighting boats) and two hundred boats full of archers, gunners, and large guns." It might have been serious for the imperial army had the plan been loyally carried out; but, fortunately for it, there were jealousies between Jānī Beg's leading men strong enough to frustrate Khusrau Khān's tactics. For some reason Khusrau Khān was unpopular with the other principal officers, and this occasion was seized to gratify ill-will by failing in the promised co-operation and exposing him to defeat. When at

[126] Mīr M'aṣūm, who had a command in the imperial army in this campaign, says nothing of a *re*-crossing, and from his narrative (here much too meagre) it might be supposed that the imperialists marched down the right bank, but the subsequent course of events seems to show that they moved on Jānī Beg along the left bank.

[127] This is the number given by Nizāmu'd-Dīn in his Ṭabaqāt-i-Akbarī; but the strength of the flotilla is very likely understated with a view to enhance the merit of the victors in the engaagement that presently took place.

daylight he found himself in the neighbourhood of the imperialist camp and climbed his mast to ascertain the position of the promised land force, he found to his vexation that not a man of that force had arrived. After waiting for a considerable time in the hope that accidental delay and not deliberate intention was causing the failure of his plan, he at last realised the truth; but still undaunted, and with the odds now so greatly against him, he resolved to attack with the fleet alone. On arriving at the sandbank above described, he opened fire on the imperialists' position, hoping probably to force a passage past it and get at the Khān Khānān's flotilla. Here, however, he was met by the return fire of artillery most likely much heavier than any his fleet could carry, and directed from a point of vantage that must have given it great superiority. Still the action lasted from sometime in the afternoon till dark with no decisive result. At night the Khān Khānān sent a body of troops across the stream to take up a position on the sandbank, and so bring the enemy's fleet between two fires. A little later an attempt to surprise his camp was made by a party of Jānī Beg's forces which had hoped to find the imperialists off their guard; but the latter were on the alert and repelled the attack. The next morning Khusrau Khān renewed the attack, this time directing it against the detachment on the sandbank, and receiving unexpected assistance from the clumsy gunners in the imperialist camp, who for a time sent their shot over the enemy's heads and into their own party on the bank, causing them some loss. When this error was rectified the Khān Khānān's fire told heavily on the attacking fleet, and after 7 or 8 hours spent in vain efforts to dislodge the detachment on the sandbank, Khusrau Khān was obliged to retreat. He had lost 200 men killed, and no doubt many more wounded. Seven of his war vessels were captured, and probably several were sunk. He carried out the retreat skilfully and gallantly, keeping the post of danger in the rear himself. Here he was overtaken by the pursuing fleet of the Khān Khānān, and actually captured, but in the confusion caused by the explosion of a magazine in the royal vessel he managed to escape.[128] According to

[128] The Tārikh-i-Tahirī, however, says: "Khusrau Charkas was taken in his boat along with several other vessels, when, at that moment, Charkas Daftīr, the chief of the merchants of Firang, who repaired yearly to Thaṭa from Hurmūz, came fluttering like a moth around this furnace, and, running his boat into the midst of the fray,

the Ṭabaqāt-i-Akbarī this second day's action took place on the 3rd November 1591.[129]

On the following day the Khān Khānān resumed his march southward, and took up position in front of the Būhirī intrenchments. Here no less than two months were spent in fruitless siege operations and vain attempts to carry the intrenchments by storm. Meanwhile the imperialists were harassed and their supplies cut off by the marauding Sindhians who hovered about their camp. How serious the situation had become owing to the unexpectedly stubborn and successful resistance of Jānī Beg, and the fidelity of Lower Sindh to his cause, is shown by the evident anxiety of the Emperor and the measures he took to support his commander. We learn from the Tabaqāt-i-Akbarī that while the imperial army was at Būhirī, "the emperor sent 150,000 rupees, then 100,000 rupees, then 100,000 *mans* of grain, with several (according to Budāūnī 100) large guns and many gunners to reinforce Khān Khānān. He also sent Rājā Rāē Singh, a noble of 4000, by the route of Jesalmīr.[130] At length the Khān Khānān was forced by stress of scarcity and despair of forcing the Būhirī defences to abandon the investment and resort to other tactics. He broke up his army into three divisions, sending one to resume the siege of Sēwan; another to invest *Shāhgarh*, a fort about 10 or 11 miles north of Būhirī; and with the third he himself proceeded southward to Fatḥ Bāgh and Jūn. The adoption of this plan indicates

succeeded in rescuing Khusrau from his captors; but the attempt cost both of them their lives" (Elliot, I. 288). One is glad to know that the historian is in error in stating that Khusrau Khān lost his life on this occasion. That able and gallant man lived for several years after his battle on the Indus. Blochmann (apparently on the authority of the M'aṣiru'l Umarā') mentions him as living and taking an active part in Sindh affairs long subsequent to this campaign (Translation of Ain-i-Akbari, p. 363). Khusrau Khān was the founder of the Dahgirān Masjid in Ṭhaṭa.

[129] As the Indus was then running in the Sāngra channel it is possible to fix the site of the actions at a spot rather more than 3 miles east by north from Bhiṭ Shah, where that channel is still well defined; because Mīr M'aṣūm says that the position was 6 kos, or 12 miles, from Būhirī, whither the Khān Khānān marched on the day following the second and decisive action. Būhirī is a township 10 miles north of Naṣrpūr Its old and ruined village site is still to be seen on the east bank of the long abandoned channel of the river. The present village is about three quarters of a mile north of the old site.

[130] Elliot, V. 462. One of the most important of the convoys was attacked and captured by the Sindhian guerillas. The conduct of the campaign reflects little credit on the imperialist leaders. Of the reinforcements, and the fate of the convoy, Mīr M'aṣūm, though present at Būhirī, says not a word.

great superiority of strength on the imperialist side, as otherwise it would have been a proceeding of incredible rashness. The object was to get Jānī Beg out of his impregnable position by a *ruse de guerre*. In that position was gathered all that could in any way be regarded as formidable of the fighting force of Lower Sindh; and, once fairly pushed into the open field, this could be disposed of without much difficulty. The result justified the expectation of the K͟hān K͟hānān; but he committed an error of judgment in allotting too weak a force to Sēwaṉ. That division was indeed ample to reduce Sēwaṉ to extremities in a very short time, but not sufficient by itself to deal with other contingencies of its position which were to be foreseen as probable. The siege had lasted but a few days when the Sēwaṉ chiefs wrote to Jānī Beg that unless he came at once to their relief speedy surrender was inevitable. The imperialist leader's stratagem now began to take effect. Knowing the besieging force to be weak, Jānī Beg left his entrenched camp, crossed the river, and advanced northward. This was what the Shāhgarh division was waiting for. It promptly descended on Būhirī, and destroyed all the defences which had kept the army so long at bay. But one of the great advantages of the position was that it could be rendered defensible by works so small in extent that they might be thrown up in a few hours; it was therefore necessary to provide for the contingency of Jānī Beg's attempting to recover it. The Shāhgarh division was thus held fast in its newly acquired ground, and could afford no assistance to the Sēwaṉ force. The situation of the latter was now somewhat critical. The Khān K͟hānān, then somewhere about Jūn or Fatḥ Bāgh, had received prompt information of Jānī Beg's movement, and had despatched a reinforcement towards Sēwaṉ. This detachment, says the Ṭabaqāt-i-Akbari, "marched 80 *kos* in two days"; and according to Mīr M'aṣūm, who was with the Sēwaṉ force, it joined the latter near the Lakī hills (the siege having been raised and the force being on its way to meet Jānī Beg), at some spot probably about 12 miles south of Sēwaṉ. If it started from Fatḥ Bāgh the actual distance covered in the two days would be about 100 miles; and the feat, though quite possible to light and well-mounted cavalry, was certainly extraordinary, and very creditable to the detachment. The route taken must have been nearly that of the present road along the right bank of the river from Kotrī northward, by which the detachment would be able to pass several miles clear of Jānī Beg's left in his parallel advance.[131] With this reinforcement the Sēwan̲ division amounted to 2000 men, while Jānī Beg's force was 5000 strong.[132] Meanwhile it was necessary to move forward without delay lest the garrison of Sēwan̲ should issue in pursuit and fall upon the rear of the division which was further exposed, while near the hills, to the danger of a flank attack from levies passing through the Lakī gorge. Accordingly the force marched 12 to 14 miles in a south-easterly direction, and then came upon Jānī Beg. The action began about noon by the Sindhians driving in advanced parties of the imperialists; it then became general, and was hotly contested for some hours, till at last the Sindhians broke and fled in all directions. Jānī Beg is admitted by all the authorities to have displayed great personal gallantry, and to have done his utmost to restore the fight. He appears not to have left the field till the last, when he was forced away by his attendants. He then hurried to the river, and embarking in one of his boats, dropped down to Ūnarpūr, 40 miles from the scene of his defeat.[133]

No name is given by any of the historians to the place where this action was fought, but the site can be fixed with approximation to correctness by indications gathered from Mīr M'aṣūm. We learn from him that Jānī Beg was accompanied by his fleet of boats on the advance towards Sēwan̲. He must then have marched near the river, which would probably in any case be his most convenient route. Now three centuries ago the river was running 4 to 5 miles, in some places much more, to the east of its present course in this part of the province, and as it is to be inferred from Mīr M'aṣūm that the battlefield was about 24 miles from Sēwan̲ its position must have been some 7 or 8 miles west, or north-west, of Sakarand. Then there is the distance mentioned of 20 *kos*, or 40

[131] The line of J. Beg's advance was probably by Hālā, and then rather to the left of the present road from Sakarand to the north.

[132] These are the numbers given by the Ṭabaqāt-i-Akbarī. Mīr M'aṣūm makes the imperialists only 1200 strong, while he puts the Sindhians at 10,000, not including rough levies armed with bows and arrows; but he invariably exaggerates on these occasions, and in his account of this campaign he is most untrustworthy owing to his desire to glorify the imperial side, and write what would be pleasing to the Court.

[133] In this battle Dhārū, son of Akbar's celebrated minister, Todar Mal, fought with distinguished gallantry and unhappily lost his life.

miles, from the battle-field to Ūnarpūr, a village at that time 4 miles north of the town of Matārī. This measurement fits in exactly with the other from Sēwan, and both indicate a spot a little north of Fathpur in the Sakarand Pargana as the site of the battle.[134]

Jānī Beg's position was now hopeless. The imperialist forces closed round him in the new position which he obstinately defended for some time, till famine and the proximity of the besieger's trenches compelled him to surrender. Before taking this step he sent orders to set Ṭhaṭa on fire, and, for some reason unexplained, he obtained from the Khān Khānān, who had him completely at his mercy, permission to retire to Ṭhaṭa till the close of the hot season which had now set in. This was probably in May 1592, and the battle near Sakarand must have been fought in April.

The Khān Khānān cantoned his army in and around the town of San, then 4 to 6 miles north-east of its present site, said to be its third, 30 miles north-west of the Ūnarpūr of that day. In the autumn he moved south to Fath Bāgh on the Rēn, and then Jānī Beg appeared and made his personal submission. The Khān Khānān, desirous of getting a sight of the sea, passed through the Delta to Lāharī Bandar, taking Jānī Beg with him. From that place both took boat and visited Manora, encountering a storm and apparently being in some danger from it on the return voyage. Orders were now received from the Emperor to bring Jānī Beg to the Court at Lāhor. Here he met with the cordial reception Akbar was accustomed to render to defeated and submissive rebels; the vassal himself being the sole object of consideration, and no thought given to the terrible cost of life and of misery to a wretched population at which unprovoked rebellion had been suppressed. Jānī Beg was nominally reinstated in the government of Lower Sindh, but he was not allowed to return there. Akbar kept him at Court, and Jānī Beg became a favourite. Besides having some literary tastes and being socially agreeable he was of an extremely pliant disposition

[134] The present site of Ūnarpūr, 22 miles north of Kotrī, is, according to the local tradition, the fifth which the village has occupied, and 6 miles west of that described in the text. I am inclined to think that in 1592 it was probably still farther east, and on the then main channel, a few miles west of Būhirī, but on the right bank as now. The Tuhfatu'l-Kirām says it was founded by Ḍām Ūnar (the first Sūmra prince), and in the authors' time (latter part of the eighteenth century), the river had carried away the lands of the township. These must have been extensive, as some land still remains.

in matters of religion, and he had no objection to gratify the free-thinking emperor by ready adhesion to the newly inaugurated *Dīn-i-Ilāhīy;* for which scandalous subserviency be incurred the wrath and abuse of his contemporary, the historian 'Abdu'l-Qādir Budāūnī. Temperance would seem not to have been an essential condition of the new discipleship. Jānī Beg gave way to excesses, and while with the emperor at Burhānpūr in 1599 he came to his end by delirium tremens.[135]

IX.

LOWER SINDH IN THE MODERN PERIOD.

ALL pretensions to independence on the part of the chiefs of Lower Sindh having been extinguished by the campaign of 1591-92, the conquered territory was made, as Upper Sindh had previously been made, a *Sarkār,* or subordinate division, of the Province of Multān, and Mīrzā Ghāzī Beg, son of Jānī Beg, was appointed Governor. He died while on special duty at Qandahār in 1627, and, as was supposed, by poison administered to him by the son of Khusrau Khān Charkas, to revenge some ill-treatment he had suffered. A succession of imperial officers followed at Ṭhaṭa for the next 110 years, when a chief of a tribe long settled in Sindh where, during the previous century it had acquired great notoriety, was nominated to the post.

The tribe of *Kalhora* is traditionally said to derive its origin from one *Miyān Odhānnā,* reputed to have descended from 'Abbās, the uncle of Muhammed; for which reason the tribe was known also under the name of *'Abbāsī.*[136] In the fifth generation from

[135] The best accounts of the campaign of 1591-92 are those of the "Tārīkh-i-Ṭāhirī, a local history written in 1621, and the Tarkhān-Nāma (1654-5). The "Beg Lār Nama," another local history, of a little later date, also treats of the subject and contributes some useful information. Mīr M'aṣūm is extremely meagre, though, as he took part in the campaign none was so competent to relate its details. For want of these it is now impossible to trace exactly the course of the river between Sūwaṇ and Naṣrpur at that time.

[136] In this notice of the Kalhoras I follow generally a paper by Captain James McMurdo, published in 1844, long after his death, in the *Journal R.A.S.,* Bombay. The author drew his account of the Kalhoras mainly from a work entitled *Wāqi'at-i-Sind* written by a Fakir.

Miyān Odhānnā, a body of the tribe, led by a chief named Ghor (perhaps Ghawar) Thal, immigrated from its original home in Makrān into Sindh and settled in Sīwastān, occupying a tract of country from which they expelled the tribe of Gūjar. Here the first Kalhora capital *Kahira Bēla* was founded.[137] On the death of Ghor Thal disputes arose among his sons, and one of these, named Jhūnīa, parted from the rest and led a party of his tribesmen into Eastern Sindh, where, it is said, they met with a friendly reception from the tribe of Odija, and settled in the lands of *Gambāṭ.*[138] Soon afterwards Jhūnīa married the daughter of Dhera Palla, who is described as "the independent chieftain of *Dēpal Ghanghro,*" that is, the eastern portion of Pargana Shahdādpur.[139] From this marriage, it is said, sprang the Kalhoras who became famous in Sindhian history. Jhūnīa died in 600 H. (1203-4 A.D.) From this date we may deduce the conclusion that the Kalhora immigration into Sindh occurred about the middle of the twelfth century. Muḥammed, son of Jhūnīa, moved to North Sindh where, in some part of the present Khayrpur territory, he built the town of *Jhūna Bēla.* He died and was buried at Gambāṭ. From this time nothing more is heard of the tribe till the middle of the sixteenth century, when Ādam Shāh Kalhora began to acquire notoriety by his masterful character and lawless proceedings. Passing with a number of Kalhoras into North-western Sindh, and being there joined by other people of kindred tendencies, he dispossessed the Chāndīa tribe of a large part of its lands and made a new settlement for his followers in Chānduka. The violence of the Kalhoras and their utter contempt for all rights which stood in the way of the tribal aggrandisement naturally aroused a storm of indignation among their victims, and brought down upon them the vengeance of government. A force sent from Multān chastised the tribe and took Adam Shāh prisoner

[137] The ruins of Kahira Bēla are 3½ miles south-west of the town of Bhān. The very large township of Kahirī must have been named from the capital.

[138] Gambāt (now a Tapa) is in the western part of Shahdādpur. The tribe of Odija, no doubt, founded the township of *Oḍiyaṇo* in Shahdādpur.

[139] Dēpal Ghānghro has since become *Dēpar* Ghāngro, of course because the distinctively Hindū name Dēpal (Dēvapāl) was offensive to Dēpal's converted descendants. It is probable that the tribe of Rājpar in Eastern Sindh once called them selves Rājpāl, and for the same reason modified their name when all had become Muhammedan. Dēpāl Ghāngro was most likely a Rājput. Owing to the careless way in which the name is written in Persian McMurdo read it Dibal-Kangirah.

to that place, where he was put to death. His body, brought back to Sindh by one of his followers, was buried at Sakhar, where his tomb on a lofty rock remains a conspicuous object to the present day. But as soon as the hand of superior power ceased to press, the Kalhoras returned to their high-handed and reckless ways. The remarkable thing about them was their habit of combining violence and rapine with persevering industry in the cultivation of the land. It was they who dug the Lārkānā canal called the Ghār, and first made Chānduka the garden of Sindh; and wherever they carried their lawless self-assertion they turned the wastes into productive fields and laboured hard to justify the claim that none so well as they could make a good use of ill-gotten gains. But all this brought no satisfaction to the ousted proprietors; rather, perhaps, aggravated the bitterness with which they regarded their inconsistently excellent plunderers. They besieged the authorities at Bakhar and Multān with their complaints. These responded with spasmodic displays of energy and severity. Again and again troops were sent into the district and the Kalhoras were driven out, on one occasion losing their leader Shah ʻAlī. But the ultimate result was always the same. As soon as the Government forces retired the Kalhoras returned, and resumed their violence and also their indefatigable industry on the land. Naṣir Muḥammed, the son of the slain Shah ʻAlī, succeeded to the leadership in 1657–8. In him the peculiar Kalhora characteristics were associated with a larger ambition than his predecessors had displayed. He too was attacked by the government troops, was made prisoner and sent to Delhi; but he contrived to escape, and, returning to Sindh, resumed the old policy, giving it a wider scope, and organising his resources more systematically. After the acquisition of Chānduka by Ādam Shāh the southern Kalhoras of Kahira seem to have joined hands with their northern brethren, and then all the country west of the Nārā river fell more or less under the domination of the tribe. The most powerful of the tribes which had suffered from Kalhora aggression, and the one that continued to offer it the most persevering resistance, was that of the *Panhwar*, a branch of the great Rājput tribe of Pramār (or Pūār), but long before these times converted to Islām. It occupied a large tract of country lying between Chānduka and western Sīwastān, including a long strip of the upland district bordering on the western hills. In a central position in this latter part of the Panhwar lands Nasīr Muḥammed founded a new Kalhora capital which received the name of *Gāṛhī*.[140] The site chosen is said to have been that of a former city of the Panhwars, which unfortunate people were made to feel the heavy hand of the Kalhoras in every form of injury and insult. With a view to increase his revenue Naṣir Muḥammed farmed the district of Lākhāwat, or Lākhāt,[141] from the governor of Sīwastān. This may be called the first legitimate proceeding of a Kalhora chief since Ādam Shāh had inaugurated the system of forcibly acquiring whatever the tribe wanted. It was also the first of a series of similar transactions by which the Kalhoras gradually gained wealth and extended their influence till at last they became rulers of all Sindh.

Naṣīr Muḥammed died at an advanced age and was succeeded by his son Dīn Muḥammed. Under him the reign of violence and lawlessness continued in full vigour. The Panhwars attempted to recover their lost lands, or some part of them, but only to be defeated and to find themselves in worse case than ever. Even the Court at Delhi was roused to indignation by the persevering and systematic ruffianism of the Kalhoras, and despatched an officer, one Shaykh Jahān, with instructions to exterminate them. This officer and the governor of Bakhar proceeded to carry out the mandate, but they were met by Dīn Muḥammed at Garēlo,[142] in the Labdaryā Pargana, and totally routed, Shaykh Jahān losing his life in the action. Such an insult to imperial authority was intolerable.

[140] The ruins of this town, situated in the township of the same name, are between 8 and 9 miles north-west of Kakar. Miyān Naṣir Muhammed's tomb is 3 miles south-west of the ruins. Local tradition places here a previous capital of the Panhwar tribe, and it is probable that this was the *Fatḥpur* which McMurdo says was the name of a chief town of that tribe captured by Naṣīr Muhammed just before he founded his Kalhora capital. "Gārhī" is a Sindhi word meaning *red*, and the name appears to have been given to the town in consequence of the reddish coloured soil of that part of the country. A local historian, writing in Persian, calls the place *Rēg Surkh*, or *Red Sand*. Masson, who passed by these ruins in 1839, says he was told they were called *Vrij* ("Travels," &c., vol. ii. p. 135). That name is no longer known in the locality.

[141] This district, now represented by a single township, is 15 miles south-east of Sewan, and has been for many years on the east side of the river. Whether it was still on the west side at this time (latter half of seventeenth century) it is impossible to say; but from the fact that it was then still administratively connected with Sīwastān it is probable that it had not as yet been separated from that district by the Indus. It extended south-east as far as Sakarand.

[142] Garēlo is 12 miles south-west of Lārkānā, and 7 west of Bākrānī.

Prince Muizu'd-Dīn, eldest son of the Emperor Bahādur Shāh, and governor of Multān, took the field against the Kalhoras. Dīn Muḥammed thought it prudent to bow before the storm and sent his brother to convey his submission. The prince foolishly accepted it as a settlement of the government account, and was returning home when some minor Kalhora chief, emboldened by the impression that the prince's clemency was in reality due to weakness and timidity, made a devastating raid into Māthila and Ūchh. This opened the prince's eyes to the folly of concessions made to ruffians. He turned on his path and swooped down on the Kalhora possessions. Gārhī and other towns belonging to the tribe were laid in ruins. Dīn Muḥammed fled, but on promise of pardon eventually surrendered. As however his brother, Yār Muḥammed, persisted in rebellion, and even attacked a body of royal troops and defeated it with great slaughter, Dīn Muḥammed was thrown into prison and after a time put to death.

Yār Muḥammed, who had sought refuge at Kalāt, himself submitted at a later period. The decrepitude of the imperial government was now becoming more and more marked, and compromise was the only way left with rebellion. Yār Muḥammed was pardoned, even received into favour and honoured with the governorship of the Dērajāt,[143] as well as the title of Khudāyār Khān. One of his early acts after thus acquiring a legitimate position of authority was to found the third Kalhora capital of Khudābād, 17 miles north-west of Sēwan. To his other honours was now added the governorship of Sīwī, and he received in form the Pargana of Rūpā in North Sindh. The age of high-handed lawlessness in Kalhora history had now come to an end, and Yār Muḥammed died about 1719 in the odour of respectability as a high State official, having held the chiefship of his tribe for 18 years. His son and successor, Nūr Muḥammed, was admitted by the Emperor Muḥammed Shāh to all the offices and dignities which Yār Muḥammed had enjoyed. He warred on the Dāūdputras, and acquired territory between Sindh and Multān; and twice defeated the Brāhūīs of Kalāt. In 1736 the fortress of Bakhar was made over to him, and in the following year he was appointed to the governorship of Ṭhaṭa. The entire province had now come under his rule, and he had acquired a position of

[143] The lower Derājāt must be intended. It is stated that its capital was then Shikārpur.

higher authority than had been enjoyed by any chief in Sindh since the death of the Arghūn Shāh Husayn in 1555. With him then, and in 1737, began Kalhora rule in Sindh.

Nūr Muḥammed had hardly been a year in his new position when Nādir Shāh invaded India, and rapidly advancing on Delhi occupied the capital in the early part of 1739. Then came the treaty of April in that year by which the Emperor Muḥammed Shāh ceded the greater part of Sindh to Nādir. The following version of that portion of the treaty which relates to the cession is taken from Frazer's "Life of Nādir Shāh."

"I make over to him (Nādir Shāh) all the countries to the west of the river Attok, the Water of Sind (River Indus) and Nālā Sunkra (Sāngra), which is a branch of the Water of Sind; that is to say, Peshāwar with its territories, the principality of Cabul, Ghaznawi, the mountainous residences of the Afghāns, the Hazārejāt, and the Passes, with the Castle of Bakhar, Sakhar and Khudābād; the rest of the territories, passes and abodes of the Jokias, Baloch, &c., with the province of Tatta, the castle of Rām, and the village of Terbin, the towns of Chun (Jūn), Samawali (Samāwātī) and Ketra, places dependent on Tatta, all their fields, villages, castles, towns and ports from the first rise of the river Attok, with all the passes and habitations which the above said water, with its several branches, comprehends and surrounds, as far as Nālā Sankrā where it empties itself into the sea; in short all places westward of the river Attok, and those parts, and westward of the river Sind and Nālā Sankrā, I have annexed to the dominions of that powerful sovereign. . . . The castle and town of Lahri Bandar, with all the countries to the east of the river Attok, Water of Sind and Nālā Sankrā, shall, as formerly, belong to the empire of Hindostan." (Dated at Shāhjahānābād, 4 Muharram 1152 = 2nd April, 1739.)

From the remark made in this treaty that the Sāngra "is a *branch* of the river Indus," it is clear that a considerable change in the course of the river in Lower Central Sindh had taken place during the century and a half that had elapsed since the campaign of 1591–2, when the main stream was running in that channel. The river had moved westward, and was running to the west of the town of Hālā; then, curving eastward some miles south of that town, was flowing through the *Ghalū* channel past Naṣrpūr. This was the course between the village of Ghoṭāno and Naṣrpūr, when, 19 years later, the sudden change westward occurred, taking the river several miles from the latter place, by which it had run for centuries. But the Sāngra probably still continued to flow, and the object of naming it at this point would be to include in the ceded territory all the lands lying between it and the existing main stream. The name Sāngra is never, so far as I know, used by the local historians to designate the channel of the river for any distance below Naṣrpūr, and its application in the treaty to some branch of the river throughout its whole course to the sea is more than I can explain. Probably the *Rēn* was the channel which it was intended to fix as the frontier line in Lower Sindh, and the conjecture is strengthened by the fact of *Jūn* being mentioned as ceded; for that town and its dependencies lay to the east of the Rēn, and, unless expressly included in Nādir Shāh's acquisitions, would have remained with the Delhi empire under a treaty which fixed the Rēn as the boundary. For the same reason, no doubt, Samāwātī is mentioned. The district so called was a subdivision of the Sarkār of Naṣrpūr, and included lands now in the Pargana of Muhabbat Dēra, situated to the east of the Rēn. *Ketra* I cannot identify. Both this name and *Terbin* are most probably corruptions. The "*castle of Rām*" is perhaps represented by Rām Bāgh in Karāchī, which latter place had been founded 14 years before the date of the treaty.

The cession of Sindh proved highly distasteful to Nūr Muḥammed, whose political wisdom now entirely failed him. He committed the fatal error of opposing the will of Nādir Shāh, and refusing to recognise him as his sovereign. But he was not long in discovering his mistake. Nādir was at Qābul when he heard of Nūr Muḥammed's revolt. Leaving that place at the end of November 1739, he reached Lārkānā on the 1st February following, and there learnt that Nūr Muḥammed had fled to Umarkot carrying his treasures with him. Thither Nādir pursued him, taking the route by Shahdādpur; but before he reached the desert fortress his advanced guard had defeated and captured Nūr Muḥammed, who had left the place after burying his treasure. It is said that this amounted to a *kror* in value. All had to be unearthed and made over to Nādir Shāh, who soon pardoned and released the captive, but refused to restore more than a part of the territory which Nūr Muhammed had lately ruled. The Kalhora received back Lower and Central Sindh, but North-western Sindh was transferred to the chief of Kalāt, and the northern district of the province to the Khān of the Dāūdputras. To the loss of so much territory and so large an accumulated treasure was added a crushing tribute of 20 lakhs of rupees.

The cession of the most valuable portion of Sindh to the great power on the west, and the imposition of so heavy a tribute proved to be one of the greatest calamities that its many vicissitudes of fortune had brought the distracted province. Throughout the long connection with the Delhi empire the difficulty of access to its dependency had imposed a powerful check on imperial coercion and imperial extortion; but now that it had a new master in possession of Qandahār, and controlling the Bolān Pass, the forcible exaction of State demands had become a much easier matter. The tribute was seldom paid unless troops were sent to collect it, and military distraint of course took the form of cruel harrying with fire and sword, in which the unhappy peasantry, and not the real defaulters —the provincial rulers—were the chief sufferers. For exactly a century was Sindh weighted with this liability, sometimes allowed to lie dormant, sometimes effectively pressed, always, when possible, resisted or evaded. At length, when it might be said to have ceased through inability to compel its discharge, it was revived by the British Government on behalf of its protégé, Shāh Shujā'a. Then, in 1839, the Tālpur successors of the Kalhora chief were required to pay the Durrānī successor of Nādir Shāh, a lump sum of 28 lakhs of rupees in settlement of all claims past or prospective, and so the tribute was extinguished.

On the assassination of Nādir Shāh in 1747, and the seizure of his Afghānistān territory by Aḥmed Shāh Abdāli, ceded Sindh passed to the latter. For some years, however, Aḥmed Shāh was too much occupied with greater affairs to give attention to the Lower Indus Valley, and Nūr Muḥammed took advantage of the troublous times to withhold the tribute. When at last Aḥmed Shāh appeared in person to assert his demands the Kalhora fled to Jesalmīr, and there he ended his days. His eldest son, Murād Yāb, succeeded, but, after ruling only three years, was deposed by his brother, Ghulām Shāh. Then followed a period of incessant contention between this man and his two brothers, 'Aṭar Khan and

Aḥmed Yār, till at length Ghulām Shāh gained the mastery, and was recognised as ruler of Sindh by Aḥmed Shāh in 1761.

Ghulām Shāh proved to be the most capable and vigorous of the Kalhora chiefs. He was also masterful and aggressive in the high degree characteristic of his family and tribe. Having nothing further to gain, and nobody else to put down, in Sindh, where to dispute his authority would now have been an act of rebellion against the sovereign at Qandahār, he turned his arms against Kachchha. Twice he invaded that province, winning on the first occasion (in 1763) the desperately fought battle of Jhārā; and on the second advancing nearly to the capital, and compelling the Rāo to cede the ports of Lakhpat and Basta. His original intention no doubt was to conquer and annex the province, but he was hardly prepared for the desperate tenacity of the defenders, whose Rājput blood made them truly formidable when driven to extremity. He was therefore content with the honour of victories which were dearly won, and with the slight acquisitions marking his prowess in foreign war. The events of his time which are of most interest now were the remarkable change in the course of the Indus, which took place about 1758–59, and the founding of Ḫaydarābād in 1768.

The shifting of the river's course last century was the most extensive of all the movements of the Indus bed in Sindh of which there is any record or tradition. The length of main channel abandoned was not less than 100 miles, and may have been much more; while that of the Rēn, which was necessarily laid dry at the same time, was some 70 miles. Whether there was at that time any eastward running branch higher up than the Rēn which contained water during the inundation season, it is impossible to say, but if there was it of course failed too, and the consequences to cultivation in the Eastern Delta country must have been very serious. The change was brought about by the stream's taking a sudden curve from its hitherto south-eastern direction to one almost due west at a point nearly in lat. 25° 40′ and long. 68° 31′. I was informed when at Naṣrpur several years ago that according to the account of the matter handed down there, the main stream had begun to diminish in volume where it ran by that place a few years before the old channel was finally abandoned. The new western channel was then evidently formed gradually, and the fact receives curious confirmation from a piece of information communicated to Captain F. Burton which he regarded as downright fiction. In his "History of Sindh" (p. 35), he says: "The natives of Sindh now enter, to a certain extent, into the spirit of the inquiry; and, like true Orientals, do their best to baffle investigation (of the question of changes in the river channels) by the strange, ingenious and complicated lies with which they meet it. At Ḫaydarabad an old man, when questioned upon the subject, positively assured me that in his father's time the Indus was fordable from the spot where the entrenched camp now stands to Kotree on the opposite bank of the river." Captain Burton received this information about 1845, so that the old man's father may very well have been personally acquainted with the local facts of the middle of the eighteenth century; and taking this probability in connection with the tradition at Naṣrpur, which has not less probability of truth on its side, there is no room to doubt that the "strange, ingenious and complicated lie" was a statement of actual fact. The channel by Kotrī, carrying at that time only a part of the whole volume of the river, would, in the low season at all events, be easily fordable.

This remarkable shifting of its channel brought the river for a distance, in a direct line, of 70 miles close to the western border of the alluvial land; and the erosion which has since occurred has now brought it into contact with either rock or the hard and compact soil of the strip of land sloping eastward from the hills of the Kohistān; and thus between Sēwaṉ and Ṭhaṭa there is no further room for the lateral movement of the stream.

This loss of the Rēn stream was in some degree compensated by a new branch, known as the Phulēlī, which, leaving the main river 10 miles north of Ḫaydarābād, runs southward along the eastern side of the low ridge of hills called *Ganjo Takar*, and, crossing the deserted channel of the Indus, falls into the old course of the Rēn, which it follows for many miles. The point at which the Phulēlī leaves the main channel may be considered a Delta head, since this arm does not rejoin the Indus, but takes a separate and widely divergent course towards the sea; becoming, however, a mere irrigational canal, and acquiring another name (*Gūnī*) before it has gone very far. Accordingly, English commentators on the history of Alexander's expedition like to fix the site of Patala at Ḫaydarābād, owing to its being near a Delta head; never dreaming that the Delta head dates back no farther than last century, and forgetting, too, that the eastern branch of Alexander's time was a "*great river*" while the Phulēlī is quite a small one.[144]

It must have been owing to the formation of the Phulēlī channel that Ghulām Shāh decided to found the new and greater capital which he named Ḫaydarābād. He had previously built Ḵhānoth, a mile south of old Hālā, in 1759-60, and later, abandoning this place, perhaps because it was in danger of being carried away by the river, he founded Shāhpur in 1762-3.[145] The expediency of establishing a capital in a position where it would be absolutely secured from the risks to which towns on the Indus banks are exposed, must have been forcibly impressed on the mind of G͟hulām Shāh by the destruction of Murādābād, the capital founded by his elder brother, Murād Yāb, during his short tenure of power. This town, which was somewhere near Naṣrpūr, was overwhelmed by a flood in 1756-7, on which occasion Murād Yāb and his two sons, escaped in a boat, and, going northward, built a new capital, named Aḥmedābād, in the eastern part of the present Sakarand Pargana. It is probable that this flood was either a consequence of the extensive changes in the river channels then beginning in that part of the country, or that it was itself the principal cause of those changes. In any case that district was evidently one that could offer no site promising the needful immunity from the danger of sudden destruction. On the other hand, the plateau of the Ganja Ṭakar, lying far above the reach of the highest inundations, and with its rocky base now washed by the recently formed Phulēlī, satisfied every condition of security and convenience. Here then the Kalhora ruler decided to erect the fortress of his new capital on the site of

[144] A friend, W. J. Wilkins Esq., late of the Revenue Survey Department in Sindh, a gentleman who has given much attention to the ancient hydrography of the province, informs me that the Phulēlī is quite an ancient branch channel, and he thinks that originally it left the main river near the village of Sēkhāt, 9 miles north-east of its present head, the portion of the channel between the original and the present head having since, as he appears to suppose, been carried away by the river. But there is not, so far as I am aware, the slightest evidence to support this theory which, even if true, would not prove the Phulēlī to be an ancient channel; since the main channel at Sēkhāt was itself comparatively modern, being the last, at this point, in which the river ran before changing to its present course in 1758.

[145] Shāhpūr, still inhabited and flourishing, is 4 miles west of Naṣrpūr.

the ancient Nīrūn, which had then come to be known as Nīrūn Kāfirī, or "Nīrūn of the Infidel times." The old stronghold was now a ruin, and its walls had sunk into shapeless heaps of rubbish. The surrounding plateau had long since been chosen as the last resting-place of certain Pīrs, or persons of saintly reputation, and, in accordance with Muhammedan superstition, the spoṭ had consequently become a specially favoured burial ground. Ghulām Shāh had the whole cleared away, showing no more respect to the dust of venerated Pīrs than to the relics of old Nīrūn; and on the spacious site thus prepared he built the fortress which he named Haydarābād. This, the last and greatest of Kalhora foundations, was begun in 1768, and became the chief's residence in 1770. He was not destined to have a long tenure of it. On the 1st August, 1772, he was suddenly smitten with paralysis, apparently brought on by his excesses, and on the following day he was dead. Popular opinion attributed his fate to the wrath of the saints whose graves he had desecrated in building his fortress.

Ghulām Shāh was the last representative of Kalhora strength of character and governing ability. He had a full share of Kalhora unscrupulousness and cruelty, but his strong hand was felt everywhere throughout the country, and he could at least provide that the privilege of wrong-doing should be confined to himself. With his death this soon came to an end, and once more the province was plunged into all the horrors of anarchy. His son Sarāfrāz Khān succeeded to his honours, and, following the early policy of his father, invaded Kachchha, as it seems, in mere wantonness and greed of plunder. After his return from an expedition unfortunately too successful, he proceeded to clear his path of those whom he suspected, as his father also had suspected, of disaffection and an ambition inconsistent with the continuance of Kalhora rule. The Baloch tribe of Tālpur had, like the Kalhoras themselves, immigrated into Sindh from the countries bordering on the west, but at a much later period. Like the Kalhoras too they had settled in Lower Central Sindh, and in the near neighbourhood of that Gambāṭ where Jhuniā Kalhora had made his home and his alliance with a Sindhian chief. The Tālpurs are said to have had very humble beginnings, and to have been simple shepherds when they were first known in Sindh. How they rose to the eminence subsequently acquired by them is not known. Their first acknowledged chief in Sindh was Mīr Shahdād, who founded Shahdādpur. His son Mīr Bahrām became the Chief Minister of Nūr Muḥammed Kalhora, and held the same office under Ghulām Shāh. The latter, however, for some reason unknown, came to dislike him, and probably to suspect him of disloyalty. Under the influence of these feelings he at last dismissed him. Sarāfrāz Khān went farther and procured the assassination of both Bahrām and his son Sobdār. But not long afterwards Sarāfrāz, proving unacceptable to the Sindhian chiefs, now in a position to set up and pull down at their pleasure, was deposed. The same fate—or perhaps good fortune—befell the next successors, and then Ghulām Nabī, a brother of Ghulām Shāh, was elected to the chiefship. At this time Mīr Bijār Tālpur, another son of Mīr Bahrām, who had long been absent on a pilgrimage to the holy places, returned to Sindh and summoned the Baloch tribes to aid him in avenging the death of his relatives. Ghulām Nabī met him in the field and was killed. His brother 'Abdu'n-Nabī shut himself up in the fort of Haydarābād where he got rid of three probable rivals by murdering three of his near relations. Mīr Bijār laid siege to Haydarābād, but, finding it too strong for him, he came to terms with the bloodthirsty 'Abdu'n-Nabī whom he acknowledged as chief of the State on condition of being himself appointed chief minister. In negotiating with such a monster Bijār sealed his own fate, 'Abdu'n-Nabī dissembled, bided his time and then hired two assassins from the Rājāh of Jodhpūr. These men approaching Mīr Bijār, under pretence of presenting a petition, plunged their daggers into him, killing him in an instant, and were then, as they quite expected, themselves despatched on the spot. Knowing what he might expect from the Baloch in return for this last deed of blood, 'Abdu'n-Nabī fled to Kalāt, whence he returned with a force which was promptly defeated. He next fled to Jodhpūr, and obtaining troops from the Rājāh returned to Sindh to be again completely defeated. Lastly he fled to Qandahār and threw himself on the protection of Tīmūr Shāh. Meanwhile since the murder of Bijār the government of Sindh had been carried on conjointly by his son Mīr 'Abdu'llāh and his nephew Mīr Fath 'Ali. It was now the turn of these chiefs to fly. In 1781, or 1782, Tīmūr Shāh sent an army under the command of Madad Khān, one of his principal officers, to reinstate the Kalhora chief. The Talpur chiefs, not yet strong enough to resist the power of their sovereign lord, bent before the storm and fled to the deserts. Madad Khān, whose memory is infamous in Sindh to the present day, let loose his troops on the devoted province and passed from north to south in one broad path of plundered and burning towns and villages and slaughtered people till even savage Paṭhāns were satiated with blood and ruin. 'Abdu'n-Nabī was reinstated and Tīmūr's army retired, but a terrible famine, accompanied with pestilence, followed as a consequence of Madad Khan's devastation, and the misery that fell on the unhappy people, who had little cause to be interested in the quarrels of the rival chiefs contending for the right to rule them, exceeded anything recorded in the previous history of the province. "The province of Sindh," wrote Elphinstone in his "Account of Qābul," is said not yet (in 1815) to have recovered from what it suffered on that occasion.

Mir 'Abdu'llāh Tālpur, with a disregard of experience which seems almost incredible, now returned to Sindh and submitted to 'Abdu'n-Nabī, who soon afterwards put him to death. The Tālpurs again rose and, led by Mīr Fath 'Alī, attacked and drove out 'Abdu'n-Nabī. The latter once more obtained a force from Qandahār, but happily for Sindh, a much less formidable one than that which had been led by Madad Khan. 'Abdu'n-Nabī was decisively defeated and compelled to fly from Sindh, whither he was never to return. So ended Kalhora rule. In 1793, the Talpurs, who had virtually ruled since 1783, received recognition from Zemān Shāh, king of Qābul, and then, Kalhora pretensions being finally ended, the vexed and exhausted province was left to recover prosperity under the milder and more benevolent rule of the Tālpur chiefs. The Kalhoras had thus held power as governors of Sindh for 46 years; namely, from 1737 to 1783. Their successors, who agreed among themselves to divide the province into the three governments of Upper, Central and Lower Sindh, held this power for 60 years, the period of rule by native chiefs closing with the British conquest of Sindh in 1843.

APPENDICES.

A.

THE *LONIBARE* MOUTH OF THE INDUS.

CAPTAIN McMURDO and Sir Alex. Burnes, in treating of the Indus Delta and the Ran of Kachchh, made some observations on the *Luni* river, which I regret to have overlooked till it was too late to refer to them in the Memoir. The former, in his article on "The River Indus," in the "Journal of the R. A. Soc.," vol. i. p. 40, says: "that the *Lonibare* of the ancients is the *Lakpat* river, *which is still known by the name of the Loni*, may without much credulity be admitted." Elsewhere he states (I am unable to recall the reference) that the name *Kori*, which is that by which the Eastern Indus mouth is now usually known, attached to it in consequence of its running by some cape, or other prominent feature of the S.W. portion of Kachchha, which was so called. This, then, makes it absolutely certain that the *Lonibare* of Ptolemy is the *Korī*, or *Lakhpat river*, of modern times. McMurdo says that: "*Bārā* is the Indian name of a roadstead, or the entrance to a harbour: it also signifies 'to the sea-ward.'" I have some indistinct recollection of the word being used in this sense along the coast of Western India. In Sindh the word *ḅārī* (spelt with the peculiar *explosive b*) means "a portion" or "division," and in its most frequent use is applied to the small square plots made by cultivators in their fields in order to facilitate irrigation.

In regard to the course of the Lūnī in the Ran I am glad to find that the conclusion at which I have arrived is identical with that of Burnes, who had far better opportunities of forming an opinion on the point. Speaking of the waters of this river he says: "I am inclined to believe that their more probable course would be towards the Indus, across the present *Runn* . . . . so that they would enter the sea by *Lacpat*." He adds: "Some of our maps have given a dotted line representing the course of the *Luni* river as I have now stated, but it must be purely supposition, as there is no channel now discoverable anywhere throughout it, and I speak from personal observation." ("Memoir on the E. Branch of the R. Indus and Runn" in "Trans. R. A. S." iii. 573.)

B.

THE MĀMŪ'Ī PREDICTIONS.

A full account of these predictions is given in the fourth chapter of Burton's "Sindh." There the celebrated Fakīrs are called *Sāmo'ī* (from the name of the first Sama capital); *Māmo-ī* (said to mean "Cannibals," or else "revealers of hidden things"), and *Haft Tan* (= "seven trunks," in reference to the headless condition of the Fakirs when they uttered their predictions). In a Sindhī copy of these predictions which is in my possession it is said that the original and true name was *Mu'immā*, and that ignorant people have turned this into *Māmū'ī*. The meaning of the word Mu'immā is *Enigma*, and certainly no name could be more appropriate to the utterances which, dating probably from the latter part of the fourteenth century, survive at the present day with undiminished interest for Sindhians. But not all of the so-called Māmū'ī predictions now current in Sindh can be accepted as genuine. There is pretty clear evidence, for instance, that the mystic art to which probably the Sūmrā of the fourteenth century resorted in order to vex and frighten his successful Samā rival, was brought to bear against victorious Tālpurs by discomfited and ousted Kalhoras at the end of the eighteenth century, and that Talpurs, quite as expert as their foes in the invention of ancient prediction, retorted in similar fashion. Thus when we find a prophecy to the effect that "sovereignty shall be snatched from Kalhoras," and another declaring that "a thin gray horse shall come from the north, and shall dash down the throne of the Tālpurs," we have no difficulty in deciding to whom their authorship, and to what period their date, may be assigned. Burton has judiciously limited his selection to those predictions which seem to have the fairer claim to be considered ancient, rejecting others which are obviously inventions or modifications of recent times. The former, or most of them, are very likely as ancient as the uncritical Sindhian believes them to be. For one of these I think I have satisfactorily accounted in the Memoir (n. 109, p. 88). Others possess a like interest from their reference to the Indus or its branches. The first in order of utterance is the well-known one relating to the channel at *Aror*, and to the *Hākro*.

> "The dyke (or bridge) of Aror shall burst.
> The Hākro shall flow.
> *Bihu*, fish and *loṛh*
> Shall come as delicacies to the Samā."

The *Bihu* is the root of a kind of lotus which affects swampy lands. The *Loṛhu* is the tuber (somewhat like a nut in appearance and taste) of a water plant which grows in pools and lakes. Both are esteemed delicacies by the Sindhian *when taken by choice*, and in addition to an ordinary and generous diet, but under other conditions their consumption might indicate a time of dire famine, when the usual food-grains were not procurable by the poor. The last line of the above quatrain is therefore ambiguous, and may mean either that the Samā should acquire valued delicacies which they had not before possessed, or that they should be reduced to such straits for food as to look upon this wretched means of nourishment as a godsend. Then it is uncertain what it was that was to "burst"—whether a "dyke," or a "bridge." The word in the original is feminine (*Ḅandhi*), and at the present day in Sindh always means "a bridge," though it might perhaps be applied to a very small embankment; while the word for a dam, or dyke, is masculine (*Ḅandhu*).[1] And, whatever it was, where was its exact position, and was its bursting to be the cause (which is the most natural inference from the language of the prediction), or only one of the consequences, of a great catastrophe? Aror itself had been deserted long before the earliest date that can be assigned to any of these predictions. If any protective embankment had been constructed in the vicinity of the ancient capital it must have had for its object the restraining of the river from reverting to its old course by Aror and its confinement to the Bakhar channel. The prediction then would point to some unusually high flood which broke into the Aror channel and also into that of the Eastern Nārā, or Hākro, and may have had calamitous consequences (or, it may be, beneficial[2]) for the population of lower Sindh. Burton says it has not been fulfilled. He, indeed, renders the first line: "The Hakro shall become a *perennial* stream," but the original merely says that it "shall *flow*," and as it is a flood-channel and "flows" whenever the flood-water of the Indus rises beyond a certain point the prediction was a very safe one to make, and to this extent it has been amply fulfilled.

Another prediction refers to the Baghār channel of the Delta. An ancient name of this was *Ār;* hence the shrine on its left bank some thirteen miles S. of Ṭhaṭa is named *Pīr Ār.*

"When, after long flowing, the Ār shall dry up,
Then shall the Baloch be held cheap."

The second line runs literally: "Then shall the children of the Baloch be sold for five *dams*" (a coin of very small value). The mention of *Baloch* indicates, I am afraid, that this prediction is not to be ranked as original and genuine. In the fourteenth century any Baloch that were in Sindh must have occupied a position of small importance, whereas this minatory utterance seems to point to downfall from superiority of some

[1] There was once a bridge across the channel at Aror, but I think it must have been built after the main stream had passed to Bakhar, and only for convenience during the flood-season when probably a branch stream continued to flow for some years subsequent to the great change in the course of the Indus.

[2] If any truth underlies the legend of the Māmūʾī Fakīrs we may take it as probable that the predictions were conceived in a spirit of hostility and menace to the Samās, and it is therefore likely that calamity rather than good fortune would be foretold as in store for them.

kind, and does very likely express the hopes of a downfall of Baloch domination entertained by many at a much later date.

The following seems to have better warrant for its antiquity:

> "Come, ye people, and dwell in the shelter of *The City*:
> Beyond the Purān build yourselves no more huts!"

Another reading inverts the exhortation, making it: "Abide not in the City: go beyond the Purān, &c." That above given is probably the true version, and I think it may be explained as a summons to the Samā of the Eastern Delta country to abandon that district and migrate to the new capital and the Western Delta. For by "*Nangar*" (a Sindhī corruption of *Nagar*), above translated "The City," Ṭhaṭa is certainly intended. It was *the* city *par excellence*, and it is still, in its fallen estate, called *Nangar Ṭhaṭa*. This prediction is no doubt a genuine production of the fourteenth century. Others foretelling calamities for the Samās and the political downfall of the tribe may be placed in the same category. Many more current in Sindh and, from their mystic jingle, dear to the people, are spurious and of comparatively recent composition. They mostly indicate a curious inability on the part of the inspired to discern the political signs of the times. Here is one that might be called, in geological language, of "sub-recent origin." The date is supposed to be of the *Samwat* era, and is borrowed from a Panjābī prediction (See Burton's note, p. 388):

> "In the year '97 the Persians shall arrive:
> They shall overwhelm Sakhar, Bakhar and Rohrī:
> They shall plant their spears in Nīrūnkoṭ:
> After this shall appear the hosts of the Mahdī."

Here we have the utterance of some pious Muslim, despairing of Sindh's ever emerging, during the present dispensation, from the evil round of new masters and new forms of calamity, and looking forward to the Islamic restoration of all things.

C.

ON THE GENERAL COURSE OF THE INDUS IN SINDH IN ANCIENT TIMES.

According to the surveys which have been made during the last half century the Indus, we find, pursues from the confluence of the Panjuad, in Lat. 29°, Long. 70° 35′, a very uniform S.W. direction for nearly 300 miles (river distance) till it reaches Lat. 26° 56′, Long. 67° 53′. About 215 miles of this great reach are in Sindh. At the point last mentioned the river changes its general direction to one due south and, maintaining this for about 60 miles, it strikes, in Lat. 26° 20′, Long. 67° 55′, the eastern base of the Lakī hills, just under the peak called *Bhago Ṭoro.* Below this point the westing movement of centuries has now brought the stream to the extreme edge of the alluvial land, and into contact with the gravel slopes bordering the Kohistān. As the gravel tracts project in a bow into the alluvial land of Lower Sindh the river, unable to erode them, is forced to conform to their contour, and to run in a great curve for nearly 180 miles to Ṭhaṭa. This curve continues through the Delta to the sea, so that from *Bhago Ṭoro* to the river mouth the course of the Indus forms an arc of some 260 miles, of which the chord is about 160 miles and the maximum depth nearly 50 miles. The general result is to give the course of the river in Sindh the form of the letter S. And, as its abandoned channels attest, such has been the form in which the river has run in past ages as it approached the sea. The lower curve of the S had a stil bolder sweep eastward, when the river ran far east of its present course unchecked by rock or gravel bed, than it has now when this part of the course has been shaped by a resistance which the current cannot overcome. Exactly correspondent was the course of the *Hākro.* The "lost river," bending at Derāwar in Bahāwalpur, from its previous W. by S. course, kept, like the Indus, a due S.W. direction for a direct distance of 180 miles, till it touched the southern end of the Khayrpur ridge. Here it came upon the tract of sand-hills which extends for 60 miles below that ridge, and was deflected due south for a distance of 50 miles to about the latitude of Sēwaṉ.[3] It now turned and ran S.E. for 100 miles when, resuming the normal direction of S.W., it flowed for 140 miles to the sea through the Korī Creek. Thus the Hākro also took the S form in Sindh, shaping its curves in remarkable conformity with those of the Indus. In the case of the former what caused the peculiarity of its course is apparent. It was the rebound occasioned by the check to its general direction met with in the sand-hills. In the case of the Indus the cause is not equally obvious. If the original S.W. direction had been kept only a short distance further the river would have run towards *Johī*, 24 miles N.W. of Sēwaṉ, then it would have been turned by the gravel fringe of the hills so as to make it occupy the bed of the Manchur lake, follow the line of the Aral and run north of Sēwaṉ towards Daulatpur, whence it would have made a wide sweep eastward before turning south towards the sea. Why the river, instead of taking this, the seemingly natural, course, turns from S.W. to due S. soon after passing the 27th parallel; why it did the same in about the same latitude when its channel lay far to the East, it is not easy to understand. Rivers have their great oscillations, extending sometimes to hundreds of miles, as well as their

[3] The channel of the Hākro has in many places been much obliterated by blown sand, and to some slight extent, no doubt, altered by the action of the Nārā floods. It is probable that when the "lost river" was flowing it curved out westward a little through the sand-hills instead of running due north and south like the present Nārā channel.

smaller ones of two or three to ten or twelve miles, and the shaping of their course at any given point is largely determined by the action of the stream at great distances higher up. However explained, this S-shaped course of the river in all ages should be remembered in considering questions of ancient local topography such, for instance, as that of the site of Patala. It will then be seen to be impossible that the river can have run at the same period in its present course near H̲aydarābād and, lower down, through the Ghāro, or ancient Sindh Sāgara; also that if Patala was at H̲aydarābād the western river mouth of Alexander's time must have lain, not at the western extremity of the sea face of the Delta, but much to the east of that point.

As regards the secular lateral movement of the river westward, it is to be observed that this has not been absolutely constant; for if the greatest number of abandoned channels are found to the east of the existing course, there are also some to the west of it.[4] A notable instance is that of the *Sindh-D̲horo* (= "Indus Channel"), which is still well defined and traceable for 50 miles from a little below Kasmor on the frontier, its course being parallel to that of the river as it now runs, and at a distance of 5 to 7 miles from it. Thus in considering the question of the river's course when Alexander saw it, it is impossible to feel sure that all parts of that course lay to the east of the present one, though there is a strong presumption that this was so. The accounts of the great expedition have come down to us in a form so condensed, and with such insufficiency of geographical detail, that to attempt to map out the Indus Valley of that time is a hopeless task. Most inexplicable is the absence of any reference to a *second* river in the valley, though the "lost river" must then have been flowing, and at no distance from the line of operations. Indirect evidence of its existence—if evidence were wanted—is perhaps to be found in the description given of the territory of *Mousikanos*. His lands were reported to Alexander as being "the most flourishing of all in India,"[5] a report verified by the subsequent experience of the Greeks. It has been

[4] The action on currents of air and currents of water produced by the difference of velocity of the earth's rotation at the Equator and at the Poles, which, in the first case, gives their special direction to the trade winds, and, in the second, causes eroding rivers to attack one particular bank more than the other and to push their beds sideways, is sometimes called "Baer's Law" from the name of the physicist Karl Ernst von Baer, who was the first to perceive it, at least in the case of running water. This action gives rivers in the Northern Hemisphere a tendency to attack their right banks, and those in the Southern a tendency to attack their left banks; but it is liable, as von Baer pointed out, to be "disturbed and modified" by that other natural law which forces rivers to oscillate in their courses, also by the effect of exceptionally strong currents, and no doubt, too, by other causes which have still to be investigated. Von Baer's treatise on the subject forms No. 3 of his "Studien aus dem Gebiete der Naturwissenschaften," and is entitled "Über Flüsse und deren Wirkungen" (On Rivers and their Action), Brunswick, 1886. 2nd edition.

[5] (Anab. VI. 15) "Of all in India" then known to the Greeks, is to be understood. So when we read that Peithon was put in charge of the Lower Indus Valley "*with all the coast* τῆς Ἰνδῶν γῆς," it is clear that no more than the coast of Sindh must be understood in spite of the wide-reaching expression.

usual to identify this territory with the district around *Aror*. I am inclined to place part of it, at all events, farther north, and to identify the whole with the south-west portion of the Bahāwalpur territory, and perhaps a considerable part of modern Sindh east of the Indus. In the northern portion of this district, and some 35 miles distant from the Sindh frontier, are the ruins of the very ancient town *Māū*, a name which at least suggests a possible connection with *Mousikanos*. The last syllable of the latter name is certainly a Greek suffix, as are the last syllables in *Oxykanos* and *Portikanos*, names which appear to have been applied to the same person through some error or confusion on the part of either Arrian or Diodorus. The meaning of all three would be "Chief of the tribe, or country, of *Mousika*, *Oxyka*, *Portika*."[6] Lassen says that *Mushika* is the name of a tribe mentioned in the Vishnu Purān, and it is possible that it may have been settled on the Indus banks; but whether or no, and however doubtful the connection between *Māū* and *Mousikanos*, it is more likely that the Bahāwalpur district would be exceptionally remarkable for its flourishing condition than the country in the neighbourhood of Aror, a very large area of which is occupied by rock and sand-hills. That the former may have been justly described in Alexander's time as ευδαιμονεστάτη is quite intelligible when we remember that it was a tract of very fertile land watered by *two* fine rivers. It is still productive, though now far from populous, and it is exposed to floods from the Indus, which in these later ages is charged with the whole volume of the Panjāb streams, while in the olden time a considerable portion of the burden was borne by the "lost river." The town of *Māū* was evidently at one time on the bank of the Indus, as were also those other ancient foundations, *Sēorāe*, nearly 30 miles to the S.W., and *Māthila* in Sindh, 38 miles still farther in the same direction.[7] All three are nearly in a line parallel to the course of the river which now runs 12 to 15 miles west of them.

[6] If the commentators had but known that there is actually a district called *Burdika*, and in the very place that would suit for the country of *Portikanos*, how eagerly would they have caught at the identification! The unlucky thing is that the *Burdī*, who have given the district its name, are, or claim to be, a *Baloch* tribe, and the immigration of the Baloch into the Indus lands is supposed to have occurred in quite modern times. Certainly the correspondence, both as regards name and position between ancient and modern, is startling enough to tempt us to enquire whether all are Baloch who say they are, or whether we are really so fully informed on the question of Baloch beginnings in India as we imagine. General Cunningham, with nothing like so much to tempt him, connected the *Massanæ* of Diodorus with *Mazārka*, a district on the right bank of the Indus, below Mithankot, but the Mazārī also are Baloch and modern arrivals on the Indus. *Burdika*, too, is on the right bank, extending for a few miles along the river, and about 30 miles north of Sakhar.

[7] A very interesting article on these and other sites in the neighbouring country by Colonel B. R. Branfill, R.E., will be found in vol. xi. of the "Indian Antiquary." Colonel Branfill accepts the local statement that *Māū* is a corruption of *Mūy* (a "hair"), the place having had, like Rohrī, the honour of being made the receptacle of a hair of Muhammed's beard. I will not affirm that the local theory is a figment of Muhammedan imagination but only that if the name of the place was really *Māū*

If the Indus flowed by Māū and Māthila twenty-two centuries ago, as is not unlikely, but by no means established, it is extremely probable that its course farther down would be by Aror, as inspection of the map will show. By some, indeed, it is considered that the gap in the hills at Aror is not wide enough to have formed a bed for the whole body of the Indus waters, and consequently that the river must have forked before reaching the latitude of Aror, and have passed through the limestone ridge by more than one opening. The Aror gap certainly strikes one as extremely narrow for an Indus main channel. At the site of the old capital it is barely 1900 feet wide, but of course much depends on its depth. If the alluvium which now fills the gap is shallow, it is difficult to see how the above objection can be answered; but if the rock lies deep below the surface, the whole stream—then of considerably less volume than it is now—may have passed through the Aror opening. The silence of Alexander's historians as to any branching of the river higher up than Patala is not an argument to which the slightest weight can be attached, since that silence was equally preserved in regard to known geographical facts of far more importance. Nor does the evidence of later times, while it certainly seems to prove that the main river, at all events, passed through the Aror gap, by any means exclude the theory that a branch-stream flowed farther to the west. It is not only possible that such a branch existed without ever being mentioned in early or in later writings, but it is not at all improbable that it still exists, and that it is the one which we know under the name of the *Western Nārā*. This stream is certainly very ancient, and it has been seen that it was flowing in the beginning of the eighth century. Its point of effluence is now probably not less than 45 miles south-west of Rohrī, but erosion of the western Indus bank has been going on very actively in this part of North Sindh during the last 30 years; and when the district around Lārkānā was surveyed 35 years ago, the head of the W. Nārā was not quite 28 miles W. by S. from Rohrī. Its head must, of course, have been still farther north in more distant times, and may have been either a little below, or not far above, Aror. In the latter case it must have occupied the present bed of the main river at Rohrī, and thence have run a few miles south and east of the present channel towards the Lārkānā district. It thus seems quite likely that in Alexander's time the main body of the Indus flowed by Aror, while a branch, of which the greater portion is still in activity, was thrown off westward and passed through the Rohrī-Bakhar gap, its bed at this point, and for

before the hair arrived there Muhammedans would be very likely to start the theory. Against the theory we must set the fact that *Māū* is far from an uncommon place-name in India, being found in the Central and North-Western Provinces; also that in Lower Sindh (in Lat. 25°, Long. 68° 57′—the region within which I think Patala is to be sought for) the extensive ruins of some ancient town bear this name. *Māū*, or *Māo*, in fact, as the learned tell us, is an ancient Aryan word, and means "the moon." It is found, in Greek characters, on the coins of *Maues*, or *Mayes*, one of the "barbaric princes" of Bactria, supposed to date 100 years B.C. (Lassen, "Zur Geschichte," &c., p. 99, and other numismatists).

these lands, or claims to rule them. His territory is at times nearly identical with modern Sindh; at times vastly more extensive, reaching northwards, if the obscure history of the period can be trusted, as far as the border of Kashmīr. In the "Tārīkh-i-Hind wa Sind" which has been so frequently referred to in the text of this Memoir, the country is called *Hind wa Sind*, and it is stated that its capital, *Alor*, was "a great city situated on the bank of the river (Sīhūn) called *Mihrān*." The period at which this history opens is approximately the beginning of the seventh century A.D, when *Sīharas, son of Sāhasī*, was on the throne. We get from it a little later an indirect indication of the course of the river for some distance below the capital about the year 632 A.D. At this time the Brahman *Chach* had acquired the sovereignty, and he was proceeding from Aror to the district called Būdhīya, on the right bank of the river, in order to suppress the revolt of certain chiefs against his authority. He crossed the river, it is said, into Būdhīya, "at a place called *Dahīāyat*, which is on the border between the lands of the Samā and Alor." These indications enable us to identify Dahīāyat with *Dēhāt*, a township on the northern border of the *Kandhīāro* Pargana, which is known to have been also the border of the Samā lands. At this place, and for some distance above and below it, the old river channel still exists and is well defined. Indeed the remnants of old channels to the north and south enable us to trace the course of the river about 632 A.D., from Aror southwards for some 60 miles, with a close approach to certainty. The distance of this course from that which was surveyed some 34 years ago is on an average about 17 miles; and thus it is seen that during a period of 1228 years, the average annual westing of the river in this part of the country has been rather more than 23 yards, so that it has taken about 75 years to move a distance of one mile. This slow rate of progress seems to point to one of two things. During this period of 12 centuries, there has been either no sudden change of channel in a westerly direction, such as might have been caused by earthquake or exceptionally heavy floods; or there *has* been a shifting of channel, at least sometimes, in an easterly direction. That there was a complete, and probably a sudden change of channel at the northern end of the reach of river we are considering during the period in question, is known. The abandonment of the ancient capital, Aror, was certainly due to the river's course having changed to one 4½ miles to the west. Round an event of such importance, marvel and legend were sure to gather, and accordingly we have the story of *Dalu Rāe*, the merchant *Sayfu'l-Mulk*, and the miraculous cutting through of the gap at Rohri. There is also another legend connected with the same event related by Lieut. Eastwick, which the curious in such matters can see in his article in the Bombay Branch, "R. A. S. Journ.," I. 203, and in his "Dry Leaves." That gentleman thought he had discovered the date of the river's migration in an inscription he found in a masjid on the small island called *Khwāja Khizr*, immediately north of Bakhar. The inscription, as its chronogram attests, is one of the very oldest, perhaps quite the oldest, Muhammedan production of this kind in India, since it is dated 341 H. or 952 A.D.; but unfortunately Lieut. Eastwick's interpretation of it cannot be accepted as correct. He rendered the first half of the inscription thus:

> "When this Court was raised be it known
> That the waters of *Khizr* surrounded it";

and from this he inferred that the inscription commemorated the change in the river's course. But, as a Persian friend has pointed out to me, the true rendering is:

> "When this sublime temple appeared,
> Which is surrounded by the waters of *Khizr*."

Thus what we gain is the knowledge that either the Indus or a branch was running by Bakhar in 952 A.D. How much earlier it came there we are not told. If it was the main river that was poetically represented by "the waters of Khizr," there is ground for inferring that the change of course took place within the decade preceding 952; for the geographers El Istakhri and Ibnu Hawqil were in Sindh at some time during that decade, and both describe the river, in their maps and their text, as running by Aror. Bakhar is never mentioned by them. It is true that the translation in Sir H. Elliott's first vol. says Aror is situated "*near the Mihran*," which would be true even if the river was 4 miles from the town; but probably the word rendered "near" means actually on the bank, for Idrisi, who must have drawn his information from these writers, describes Aror as "situated *on the bank* of the Mihran which runs to the west of the town." Thus on a consideration of all the evidence it is probably safe to conclude that the change of course from Aror to Bakhar took place about 950,—perhaps a year or two earlier. As to the cause of the change there is no means of forming an opinion. If, as I have conjectured, a branch stream previously ran through the Rohri-Bakhar gap, the main river may have been drawn into its effluent during some high flood, and Aror may thus have been left waterless.

With respect to the course of the river lower down in North Sindh, it is evident, from the number of ancient channels that are found to the east of a line drawn from *Kandhīaro* through *Naushahro*, that the Indus ran for ages through the narrow tract between that line and the sand-hills of the Khayrpur territory, always with a tendency to bend due south, and then south-east soon after passing the 27th parallel. About the latitude of Sēwan, the tendency to a S.W. direction became more marked. The country for some distance around the town of *Sakarand* has evidently been a principal centre of river disturbances, for there the land is furrowed in all directions with a vast and bewildering tangle of old channels, which baffles all effort to unravel it when it is attempted to fix the river's course at any particular period. To the south-east of this point the *Lūhāno* channel is still very clearly defined for many miles. That the Indus was running in this channel in the eighth century, is to be gathered with certainty from the history of the Arabs in Sindh, taken in connection with the descriptions of the Arab geographers. From the latter we know that it was still running in that channel in the middle of the tenth century. Its abandonment was in all probability the cause of the ruin of Manṣūra, which place, though 6 or 7 miles distant from it, was yet dependent on it, and that event there is evidence to show occurred most probably at the end of the thirteenth or the beginning of the fourteenth century (see Memoir, p. 72). It is possible, indeed, that Manṣūra was deserted because of the failure of the branch-stream only, though more probable that the change of the main river to a channel farther west occasioned the calamity. Of the branch-stream in question we have a description by the Arab geographers. It left the main river near *Kalrī* (10 miles E. of Sakarand), flowed round the east side of Manṣūra, and rejoined the Lūhāno some 10 miles to the S.W. of the latter place. Its total length must have been about 50 miles. It is the only branch-stream mentioned by the Arab geographers, who in their maps lay down the course of the Indus in Sindh as a straight line, towards the southern end of which a semi-circular loop represents the branch-channel. Another branch-stream in this neighbourhood is mentioned in the Chachh Nāmā. This was named the *Jalwālī*. It ran to the east of *Brahmanābād*, and apparently close to the town. Whether it came from the Indus or the Hākro is uncertain. It may possibly have been the channel that flowed by Manṣūra, to which no name is given by the Arab geographers. The name *Jalwālī* is very possibly an old form of *Jarārī*, and, if my memory is not at fault, the *Jarārī Wāh* is mentioned in some of the local histories as a branch channel in this region. At the present time an inundation canal in the neighbourhood preserves the name, and a township in the vicinity of the site of Manṣūra is called Jarārī.

Three or four miles south of Manṣūra we come upon the most northerly remnants of branch-channels running south-east, indicating that here was the position of the most ancient Delta head now traceable. The spot is about 150 miles from the centre of the sea-face of the Delta, and at the present day some 82 feet above sea-level.[9] It is nearly 50 miles north of the position which I would assign to Patala, where the Delta-head was in Alexander's time. Between this point near Manṣūra and the latitude of Ṭhaṭa, in a space of 80 or 90 miles, some seven other sites of Delta-heads may be traced in the maps, and probably more on the ground if carefully examined. The head of the Nile Delta is said to have moved only 17½ miles seaward—from *Memphis* to *Baṭnu'l-Baqara* below Cairo—in 2000 years.[10] The immensely greater progress of the Indus Delta-head is no doubt due to the exceptionally rapid rate at which the river mouths in activity for the time being advance into the sea, though, as a whole, the Delta grows more slowly than that of the Nile. But the striking fact of

[9] The fall of the alluvial land in Sindh between Kasmor and the latitude of Sewan is *meridionally* 1 foot per mile, thence to the sea about 7⅓ inches. The fall eastward from the course of the river is about 9 inches per mile. The fall of the river-bed varies from less than 5 to rather more than 8 inches per mile.

[10] "Das Delta des Nil," von Dr. Joh. Jankó (Buda Pest, 1890), p. 268.

Lower Sindh hydrography in later times, has been the disappearance of real Delta-forming channels altogether. The extensive change of channel which took place in Lower Sindh about the middle of last century, and the subsequent lateral movement of the bed by erosion, have had the effect of greatly straightening the river's course. It is naturally at some great bend that rivers, on reaching a certain level, throw off the branch-streams that enclose deltaic areas. In the case of the Indus such a bend in the lower course no longer exists, and there is consequently no great Delta branch: it can hardly be said that there is now more than one mouth. The latest Delta-head was that formed by the river's dividing into the two streams called the *Sata* and the *Ochto*, at a spot half way between Thata and the sea. Of these, the *Sata* dried up some 17 or 18 years ago, in consequence of the artificial widening of the head of the *Ochto*, and the subsequent "sucking into" that arm of the whole volume of the river. But this was a mere miniature Delta, its depth being only about 30 miles, and its base 15 or 16 miles in length. It may be expected that this state of things will continue until by some great disturbance the river shall be forced back eastward in Lower Sindh, where, on making the inevitable bend to south-west, it will send out an arm towards the Ran of Kachchha and thus again create a real Delta. The history of the river's movements in the past teaches us that such disturbances, though rare and coming at very long intervals, may be counted on with certainty.

D

ITINERARIES IN THE LAS BĒLĀ COUNTRY:—
A CORRECTION.

The data for estimating the average length of "a day's journey" given at page 66 of the Memoir, and also the assignment of positions to the ancient places there mentioned, require correction in the light supplied by Colonel Holdich, R.E., in his extremely interesting lecture on "A Retreat from India," delivered in the United Service Institution of India in June last, a copy of which he has been so kind as to send me. Colonel Holdich has found evidence of elevation of the coast west of Cape Monze, or, more precisely, of the basin of the Purāli river, far more extensive than has hitherto been suspected—so extensive, indeed, that he considers that the coast line at Son Miānī has advanced at least 20 miles since the days of Alexander. If his identification of the ruinous site called *Khair Kot* with the *Kambalī* of the Middle Ages is correct, the advance of the coast-line must have been still greater than this, for Kambalī was only 2 miles, at most, from the sea in the middle of the tenth century, and *Khair Kot* must be, so far as I can judge, fully 25 miles from the coast. This remarkable elevation of the Purālī basin explains what has hitherto been so obscure in the account of the voyage of Nearchus. The harbours which he found along the coast have since been elevated out of existence, and their dried-up basins must now be sought for at long distances inland. Thus, too, some of the difficulties of the old itineraries may be explained. The position of Kambalī having to be put back northward a long way, the distance from that place to Armāīl, instead of being 70 miles, was probably well under 50, and, if Colonel Holdich is right as to the *Khair Kot* identification, even well under 40 miles. In either case the "two days' journey" of the itineraries is at once seen to be a correct statement of fact. As regards this identification, however, the grounds of which are not mentioned by Colonel Holdich, it must be said that there are some strong reasons for dissenting from his opinion. It seems to me that the itineraries require Kambalī to be placed far to the east of the position of Khair Kot, which is north-west of Līārī (how far Colonel Holdich does not say), and far to the east even of the latter place. I would suggest a position for it not less than 10 miles south-east from Līārī, and some 5 miles south-east of the village of *Shaykh Rāj*, which would bring it near to the depression which Colonel Holdich says was once a harbour on the coast, and is called *Sirondha*. The reason for thus locating Kambalī is that, according to the itineraries, it was only 4 days from *Dēwal*, and, even as placed by me, it would be more than 90 miles from the latter place: the stages would average 23 miles. But if it were anywhere near the suggested position the *Purālī* must have been running from 4 to 5 miles to the east of its present channel, for Kambalī was a large town, and, as such, it must, in that "*inops aquarum*" district, have been situated either on the river or some branch of it. Colonel Holdich has found dried-up channels much to the east of the existing course, so that one objection which would have been fatal to my proposal is removed. Another may remain however. If there are no ruins to be discovered, either above or below the surface, in this neighbourhood, or perhaps much farther east or north-east, the fact would certainly afford a convincing argument against the tenableness of my present view. There ought to be some relics of Kambalī in existence. Ibnu Hawqil ranks the place as, if not equal to the capital, *Armāīl*, at all events only second to it. He says, *Armāīl wa Qanbalī madīnatān kabīratān*; "Armāīl and Kambalī are two large cities."[11] *Armāīl* is supposed to survive in the modern Bēlā; the ruins of the other "great city" must be traceable. Colonel Holdich may have much better reasons for his view than I have alleged for mine, but if he has, the difficulty about the itinerary remains to be solved. I may add that there is evidence to show that Kambalī was in existence at the time of the Arab invasion in the beginning of the eighth century. At least I think there can be no doubt that this was the place referred to by Bilādhurī when he wrote that M. Hārūn (the Governor of Makrān, who accompanied M.

[11] Idrīsī, who, however, is not so good an authority as Ibnu Hawqil, says: "Kambalī competes with Armāīl in respect of size, wealth, and population" (Elliot, I. 80).

Qāsim during part of the march) died near Armāīl, and was buried بقنبل. In M. Reinaud's edition of the text of the *Futūhu's-Sind* the name appears without a single diacritical mark, but I think we may supply what under the circumstances seems to be obviously a restoration of the original pointing, so as to get the reading *bi Qanbal*, "at Qambal."

It now becomes necessary to find another position for *Manhātar*, so as to bring that place as nearly as possible into line with *Kambalī* and *Ghāro* (at the edge of the Indus Delta, by which no doubt the route to Dēwal lay)[12] and shorten stages as much as possible. Instead, therefore, of placing *Manhātar* on the Līārī at Karāchī, I would fix its position conjecturally nearly 20 miles north-east of Karāchī. The route would then cross the *Hab* river a little less than 30 miles north of Karāchī, and continue westward 20 to 15 miles north of the present route to *Son Miānī*. Thus corrected, the figures at page 66 would be as under:

Armābīl (Armāīl) to Kambalī .	2 days .	46 miles.
Kambalī to Manhātar . .	2 ,, .	48 ,,
Manhātar to Dēwal . . .	2 ,, .	45 ,,

The probability is that a long stage of 30 to 32 miles would be made from *Kambalī* eastward, on account of the scarcity of water in that part of the country, and then a short stage to *Manhātar*.

E

THE MARCH TO THE ARABIUS.

In the lecture referred to in the preceding note Colonel Holdich places the crossing of the Arabius by the Greeks at some point "not far south of *Bēlā*." If this was also the point at which their route first struck the Arabius, which, however, as Colonel Holdich observes, is not necessarily to be inferred; and if the camp on the eastern border of the Arabitæ was on the *Malīr*, as suggested at page 17 of this Memoir, it would follow that the five days' march from this latter point covered a distance of more than 100 miles, "some of which" (says Colonel Holdich) "would be heavy, though not very much of it." He considers that the difficulty is not serious, and, indeed, as a mere obscure episode in the "retreat from India," the march to the Arabius is not deserving of any very serious discussion. It will be remembered, however, that the length of these five days' marches has a bearing of some little importance on matters which have been considered in Section II. If the average rate of marching through the country of the Arabitæ exceeded 20 miles a day, there is

[12] A more direct line to Dēwal would have necessitated ferrying across the Ghāro Creek.

nothing to show why the preceding 9 days' march from Patala should have been less rapid; or, in other words, why the position of Patala should not be fixed some 70 miles further north, or north-east, than that which I have suggested. It may be well, therefore, to see whether it is not possible to construct some theory of the march that will not involve any of these difficulties. In considering the question of the probability or otherwise of such an excessively rapid rate of advance as over 20 miles a day having actually been attained, we must bear in mind the following facts:—First, the considerable strength of the force which set out on this retreat. Allowance having been made for the reduction of numbers, consequent on the detachment of Craterus, the provisions of crews for the fleet, and the garrisons left behind, the army remaining under Alexander's immediate command has been estimated by Dr. Thirlwall (in his "History of Greece") at 50,000, and by Droysen (as quoted by Lassen) at 80,000 men. Secondly, the army marched in one body—not in detachments. This is the only reasonable inference from Arrian's statement, that Alexander "set out from Patala, and advanced to the Arabius ξὺν τῇ στρατιᾷ πάσῃ," when we remember how frequently mention is made of detachments and redistributions of the army on other occasions. Thirdly, there is nothing in the narrative either of Arrian or Q. Curtius to indicate any necessity for an exceptionally rapid movement. It is not easy to see how there could be when Alexander knew that he had no more serious opposition to expect than such as might be offered by barbarous tribes. Taking all this into consideration, it seems to me that we must reject the hypothesis of a forced march of a very extraordinary character, for such, under the circumstances, it would have been, and seek some other solution of the difficulty. Colonel Holdich here supplies important aid by his remark that in those days "the Arabius may have been far to the east of its present channel—indeed, there are old channels which indicate that it was so." If there is any truth in "Baer's law," this is exactly what might have have been expected. Next, we must read the accounts of Arrian and Q. Curtius together. It is curious that the latter mentions only the *Eastern* Arabitæ; the former only the *Western*. Q. Curtius says that the tribe, after well considering the matter, made their submission to the invader on his arrival in their lands. Up to this point Alexander had made nine marches from Patala. His camp would probably be on the *Malīr*, which, in August, would no doubt contain an ample supply of running water. The position would perhaps be 7 or 8 miles E. by N. from Karāchī Cantonments. "From this point" (proceeds Q. Curtius) "he arrived on the fifth day at a river, called by the natives *Arabus*. A desert and waterless tract followed, traversing which he passed into the country of the Oritæ." This desert tract is evidently the one referred to by Arrian in describing the night march of Alexander immediately preceding his attack on the Oritæ. Q. Curtius has nothing more bearing on the present question. Where, then, did the Greeks come upon the Arabius? Following Colonel Holdich's indications, and adding, with much regret, some guesses of my own, I would place the channel of the river of those days some 5 miles east of the present one (still further east if physical facts would permit, as to which I am in complete ignorance). Then I would place the mouth of the river rather to the north of the latitude of Līārī, and would suggest that the point of arrival at the bank was about 10 miles E. by N. from Līārī, and 20 miles N., or N. by E., from Son Miāni. The distance from the camp on the Malīr to this point would be about 65 miles, and consequently the marches would average 12½ miles—a very fair rate, even if the lower of the estimates of numbers above given be considered excessive, and if it be thought probable that the real strength did not exceed that of a strong modern army corps. Then comes the question did Alexander cross the river at this point? If we had nothing but the account of Q. Curtius we should be quite certain that he did; but there is something in Arrian to suggest that he did not—even to make it almost certain that he did not, though the something is only one word. He says Alexander "advanced to the Arabius and thence (taking various selected bodies of his force) turned left towards the sea (ως ἐπί την θάλασσαν εν ἀριστερᾷ ἐτρὰπετο). How could he be said to turn his march towards the sea if he was already on the shore? If παρὰ had been used instead of ἐπὶ, all would have been clear; for "turned left *along* the sea" would have accurately described the route, bending at the Arabius from the hitherto N.W. direction to one W. by S., of any one desiring to keep near the coast, and it was Alexander's object to have wells dug for the service of the fleet, as well as to attack the Oritæ. Then if he did not cross the river where he first came upon it, how is that fact to be explained? Can a theory of the march which requires Alexander to turn *away from* the sea at this point be justified? I believe it can, and that the key to the difficulty is to be found in the flight of the Western Arabitæ. As to this Q. Curtius is silent, but Arrian says (mentioning Arabitæ now for the first time) that these people, "among the independent tribes occupying the country near the Arabius, not considering themselves equal to an encounter with Alexander, and yet being unwilling to submit, fled to the desert when they learnt that he was approaching." By the "desert" is probably to be understood the hill-country to the north. We can easily understand that the Western Arabitæ, separated from their fellow-tribesmen on the east by some extent of hill country, and perhaps not consulted by them as to the policy to be pursued towards the invaders, might refuse to be bound by the acts of their brethren, and determine to take a line of their own. As Alexander always treated flight of this kind as an act of rebellion, he would, on arriving at the Arabius and learning of the event, most probably pursue the fugitives, that is, he would turn *northwards*. Then we may suppose that after proceeding some distance—say 30 miles—he found the Arabitæ had got too far ahead, or had entered a region where it would be inconvenient to follow them, and that he turned to the more important business of the wells and the coercing of the Oritæ. A short pursuit, *ending in failure*, would very likely be thought unworthy of mention by the authorities from whom Arrian drew his information; so that the silence of the historian on the point would not be in the least extraordinary. Immediately after mentioning the flight of the Arabitæ Arrian goes on to describe the crossing of the river and the march against the Oritæ. The narrative, as it stands, is certainly in some confusion, easily explicable by the fact of Arrian's having compiled and condensed from various sources, being at the same time without any notion of the geography of the country in which these events occurred. Thus no probability will be violated if the narrative be emended so as to make the sequence of events stand in this order: the arrival of the army near the mouth of the Arabius, where Alexander learns of the flight of the Arabitæ; the pursuit of the tribe for perhaps 30 miles or so northward, along the river; the abandonment of the pursuit, the crossing of the river and *turning left towards the sea;* the night march through the desert region west of the Arabius. Thus Colonel Holdich's view as to the point of crossing, arrived at from a consideration of the requirements of the narrative in respect to the events on the west bank of the Arabius, can be sustained on other grounds; while the difficulty in regard to the excessive length of the marches to the Arabius, which seemed to be involved in that view, is got rid of. It seems to me that the farther east we can place the course of the Arabius in Alexander's day, the more intelligible will become the account of occurrences to the west of the river, and the more easily we can explain the existence at that time of a considerable "regio deserta et inops aquarum" on the right bank where now the tract of country has, I believe, become less inhospitable.

F

THE VOYAGE OF NEARCHUS FROM ALEXANDER'S HAVEN TO THE MOUTH OF THE ARABIUS.

The discovery of the great advance of the coast about the head of Son Miānī Bay since the time of Alexander enables us to explain some difficulties connected with the account of the voyage of Nearchus which hitherto have defied solution. One remarkable thing is that in this earlier part of the voyage the estimates of the courses run now begin to startle us by their accuracy, so far, that is, as in the absence of any certain identification of places on the coast it is possible to judge. For, under the new light which he himself has thrown upon the question, Colonel Holdich, it seems to me, can hardly show cause for maintaining that these estimates are excessive. I here review the narrative of the six days' voyage to the mouth of the Arabius. As to the position of Alexander's Haven, I imagine it to be indisputable that it was somewhere in Karāchī *Bay*, though probably not in that part of it now called Karāchī *Harbour*. Something depends on the identification proposed for *Krokala*. I think

Colonel Holdich attributes too much importance to the resemblance between the names *Krokala* and *Kakrālā*. It is not at all unlikely that the "sandy isle" was called *Kakrālā*, and that the Greeks turned this into *Krokala*. It has been discovered, I believe, by a gentleman in Lower Sindh that *Kakrālo* means "Land's End." That may be the recondite meaning known to a learned few, but in the vulgar Sindhī tongue *Kakro* means "a pebble," and *Kakrālo*, the adjective, means "pebbly." An island in the sea, may, therefore, have very well had that name, and have been better entitled to it than a district in the Delta, where, south of the Baghār channel, I think, pebbles are conspicuous by their absence. But *Krokala* may quite as well represent something else. Sir H. Elliot thought it might have something to do with the *Kharaks*, a piratical tribe. At all events it is certain that the district about Karāchī Bay was at the time of this voyage called, not *Kakrālā*, but *Sangada*. It is equally certain that the island *Krokala* was not a part of the Indus Delta, for, as we have seen, wherever it was, it can hardly have been less than 8 miles from the nearest river mouth; and if Colonel Holdich is right in thinking that I have under-estimated the rate of the Delta's growth, the distance must have been much greater. A glance at a chart of the coast will show that even at the distance I suppose, there might have been soundings of 7 or 8 fathoms in places between Krokala and the Indus mouths. Until, then, stronger evidence to the contrary can be produced, I think that Alexander's Haven must be placed somewhere in Karāchī Bay. The precise position can hardly be determined. I should incline to some spot about Observatory Island, which place was accessible by a "narrow creek," and where, as we are told, there was a harbour for sea-going vessels, many centuries after the time of Nearchus. A circumstance mentioned by Arrian may assist persons on the spot to form a better opinion as to the position of the anchorage than my recollection permits to me. He says that Nearchus, fearing attacks from the barbarians, surrounded his camp with a *stone wall*. Where were the stones found? My recollection is of mud flats, stoneless alluvium, and blown sea-sand. A modern Nearchus would not, indeed, find any difficulty, as stones in vast quantity are to be seen in the neighbourhood, but all brought, I believe, from a distance of 3 or 4 miles inland for harbour and railway works.[13] The point, however, is not material. Starting from, say, Observatory Island, the first run was of 60 stadia—6 to 7 miles—to a "sandy beach," which, the context shows, was part of the *mainland*, for it is said that a desert *island* lay *close* to it (ἐπῆν), under the shelter of which the fleet cast anchor. The island was called *Domæ*. Colonel Holdich is inclined to identify this Domæ with Manora, and others have taken the same view. But Manora is even now 4 to 5 miles from the nearest mainland, and must have been farther then. Moreover, it is said that the crews found fresh water on going 20 stadia—say 2 miles—*inland* (ἐς τὴν μεσογείην).

[13] But stone is found, I think, on the narrow strip of land projecting into the alluvium, which terminates at *Scandal Point*. This is only ¾ mile W. of Observatory Island.

This should be enough to put Manora out of the question. I would place *Domæ* rather more than 4 miles due west of the town of Karāchī, or perhaps farther north; it is difficult to say how far north of the present highest water mark the sea reached in those days. Here fresh water would be found within the space mentioned in the narrative. The distance is 6 miles from Observatory Island. We may assume that, being so short, the run was pretty accurately estimated. From *Domæ* a run of 300 *stadia*, lasting till night, brought the fleet to a place called *Saranga*. No mention is made of the cape now called Cape Monze, or *Rās Mūārī*, though the fleet must have rounded it in this course. Where *Saranga* was can only be conjectured by the length of the run mentioned. It seems probable that the mouth of the *Hab* river would be tried as an anchorage for the night. The distance to this point from Domæ (as above placed), measured round the coast, is about 26 miles, sufficiently approximating to the 300 *stadia* of the narrative. But the statement that the fleet anchored, πρὸς αἰγιαλῷ, seems to indicate that the spot was an open beach, and not a creek like the *Hab* mouth. In this case we may place Saranga 3 to 5 miles farther north. In favour of the *Hab* is the fact that fresh water was found at only 8 stadia (say $\frac{3}{4}$ mile) from the anchorage, that is, it might be conjectured, from a pool in the bed of the river; for the Hab is a mountain torrent, which has a continuous flow only during rainy periods, a circumstance which would account for the silence of the narrative as to any river being met with here. Then there has actually been a port in this place—a port abandoned so late as last century, in consequence of the silting up of the *Hab* mouth. Its name, too, has no slight similarity to that given to the spot where the fleet anchored. We have only to suppose that the Σ of the latter was originally Κ, and we shall have Κάραγγα, a very fair representation of *Kharak*, the name of the *Hab* port. However this may be, and it is certainly not a point to be pressed, there can be no doubt that the *Saranga* of Nearchus was either at the *Hab* mouth or a few miles farther north. In either case the estimated run would correspond very closely—in one case, indeed, exactly—with the actual distance. At this point the narrative becomes a little obscure, owing apparently to a clause or two of the original text having been omitted in the process of copying, or to some inadvertence on the part of the author. The translations of Dean Vincent and Mr. McCrindle, too, are not successful here, and tend to mislead the reader. It will be well to take the passage in the exact order of Arrian, omitting for the present those clauses which are not material to the immediate question: "Sailing thence (from Saranga) they came to anchor at *Sakala* (lacuna); and passing between two rocks they brought to in *Morontobara*, having made a run of 300 *stadia*." There is plainly a gap in the narrative where it is indicated above. There is no mention of the length of the run from Saranga, nor the usual opening of a new passage with such expressions as "sailing hence," or "On the following day they sailed;" instead of which we have an abrupt transition from the anchoring at *Sakala* to the arrival at *Morontobara*. Vincent and McCrindle have apparently endeavoured to fill up this lacuna, or at least to soften the harshness of the transition, by supplying words of their own. They have also so misread the narrative as to transfer the rocks from *Morontobara* to *Sakala*. The whole passage may be thus rendered, following the order of the text as closely as possible. "Sailing thence they anchored at Sakala, a desert place; and passing between two rocks, so close to each other that the blades of the oars on both sides touched them, they dropped anchor in Morontobara, having made a run of 300 *stadia*. The harbour was large, well enclosed, deep and calm; but the entrance was narrow. In the local tongue it was called *Women's Haven*, because a woman first ruled this country. As they were passing between the rocks they encountered great breakers and a violent current, but the fact was that to take a circuitous course wide of the rocks seemed a troublesome undertaking." McCrindle's translation runs thus: "Weighing from Saranga they reach Sakala, a desert place, and anchored. On leaving it they passed two rocks so close to each other that, &c. &c., and after a course of 300 *stadia* they came to anchor at Morontobara." Here, by inserting the words "on leaving it," and altering the order of the passage in the Greek, Mr. McCrindle puts the rocks at *Sakala*, and 300 stadia from the position assigned to them by Arrian. Vincent does the same. He says: "Weighing from thence (Sakala), they passed between two islets so near that their oars brushed the rocks on each side, and *at last* reached Morontobara after a course of 300 *stadia*." Now we know that *Sakala* was somewhere on the open eastern coast of Son Mīānī Bay, and it is thus made to appear that Nearchus (having presumably left his wits behind him at Sakala), with abundance of sea-way open to him, deliberately charged at an extremely narrow passage between rocks! Then Mr. McCrindle translates: "They thought it a great achievement to have passed those two rocks in safety, for when they were passing them the sea was boisterous and running high." And Dr. Vincent has it: "In their passage, besides the danger of the rocks, they had encountered *a severe gale*, and a very violent current, and thought they had performed wonders in surmounting the dangers that surrounded them." There is not a word about a gale, or about wind at all, in this part of the narrative, and the first mention of bad weather occurs some days later when the fleet had left the mouth of the Arabius far behind. What actually occurred was clearly this. At the end of the run Nearchus found that the harbour of Morontobara might be reached at once by the "narrow entrance" described, and, the crews being no doubt tired after their long day's row, he chose to risk this doubtful passage rather than face a more circuitous, though a safer, way in, which would have involved, as he thought, "great trouble;" for this, and not "a great achievement," or "wonders," is the meaning of *μέγα ἔργον* here. C. Müller makes the passage very clear in rendering it: "attamen extrinsecus circumnavigare ex alto *nimis ardua res* esse videbatur." The strong current and the high breakers met with in passing through were, no doubt, caused by the ebb tide's rushing out by the narrow and rocky channel. The leaving out of consideration the two highly significant particles ἀλλὰ—γὰρ, importing "the fact of the matter was that," and introducing the explanation of the dangerous choice made by Nearchus, has here led the English translators completely astray. The question of the position of the rocks is of some little importance, as it affects the identification of Morontobara. It is not said that the rocks were high, and it is quite possible that they may now be deep under sand. On the other hand, examination of the country about the Sirondha lake might lead to their discovery, and Colonel Holdich's identification would thus be confirmed.

Sakala may be placed, I think, a little east of *Bidok Lak*. From *Saranga* (say a few miles north of the *Hab* mouth) to this spot the distance would be 24 miles, and though the length of the run is not stated in the narrative we have other means of knowing, as will presently be seen, that it must have been reckoned at 220 *stadia*. The shortness of the runs in this early part of the voyage shows that the fleet was entirely dependent on its oars. We have two runs of 300 *stadia* recorded, and probably a full day's voyage would be about 10 hours, and the reckoning of progress about 30 *stadia* (3 miles) an hour. Between *Saranga* and *Sakala* the fleet must have passed an island, though the fact is not mentioned. This was *Gadānī*, now a part of the mainland. I would identify Ptolemy's Κοδάνη on the Gedrosian Coast with *Gadānī*, which is described in the Memoirs of the Geological Survey as "the most conspicuous hill on the coast," and as "peculiarly white in colour," so that it would be likely to attract the attention of passing navigators. In point of distance from preceding anchorages the position assigned by Colonel Holdich to Morontobara suits very well. I make it about 27 miles from Bidok Lak, and in the narrative it is said to be 300 *stadia*. From Morontobara to the mouth of the Arabius the run was 120 *stadia*. It is not certain, but probable, that the 70 *stadia* stated to be the length of the inshore channel by which the sea was reached, are included in this reckoning. It may be, by the way, that this channel was the usual and the safest means of access to Morontobara, and resorted to by vessels coming from the north; while some miles farther south there was a short cut, but a dangerous one, into the harbour. It is easy to understand how strong the temptation to run the risk would be to Nearchus—generally so cautious—and his tired crews when it was found that the alternative was to go round (ἐκπεριπλῶσαι) by this long channel. It may be noted that when they left this channel at daylight the tide is said to have been running out, a confirmation of my view that it was running out when the fleet arrived at the "narrow entrance" the previous afternoon or evening.[14] The whole description here points to the probability of considerable physical changes being at that time in progress. The spacious harbour had no doubt been gradually encircled by a belt of sand-dunes, and the action of the tide had kept a connecting channel open for some miles along the shore. It had also no doubt kept open a more direct communication with

[14] So dangerous a passage would hardly have been attempted after dark.

the outer sea at some spot where perhaps the sand-belt was narrow, and where there were *rocks*.

From Morontobara, if that is identical, as Colonel Holdich has no doubt, with *Sirondha* lake, to Līārī, where he places the mouth of the Arabius in those times, the distance appears to be 10 miles, a sufficiently close correspondence with the 120 *stadia* reckoned by the navigators. The harbour at the river mouth is described as "spacious and good," but it is not said that it was deep, as was reported of Morontobara. Is there any depression near Līārī similar to that of Sirondha? Its non-existence would not, of course, invalidate Colonel Holdich's identification, since there has been plenty of time for a spacious harbour to be silted up to the level of the surrounding country. The process of physical change which has here been so remarkable would also leave no trace of the island which was near the harbour; but as the island was noted as being "high," it might possibly be recognised in some isolated hill in the neighbourhood.

It has been said above that it is possible to supply the missing reckoning of run between *Saranga* and *Sakala*, and that this was 220 *stadia*. We find the omitted reckoning by means of the estimate, given a little later, of the total length of the course along the coast of the Arabitæ territory which is stated to be 1000 *stadia*. The question has been raised, indeed, as to the point from which this measurement is to be taken, because Arrian says that it was from the place whence the fleet started (ἔνθενπερ ὡρμήθησαν), and the original starting-point was the naval station on the Indus. If we suppose the latter to have been intended we find the sum of runs *recorded* to be

(*a*) Between the Naval Station and Alexander's Haven	.	300 *stadia*
(*b*) Between Alexander's Haven and the Arabius	. .	780 "
	Total	1080 "

To which must be added an estimate of the *unrecorded* runs:

(*a*)	70 *stadia*	
(*b*)	220 "	290 "
	Total	1370 "

So that the statement of the length of the *paraplus* would be below the probable truth, according to the writer's own data, by 370 *stadia*, a very important discrepancy. But it is to be remembered that the writer expressly states that the *paraplus* of which he gives the length is that along the "Coast of the Arabitæ," and also that he has previously described the fleet as coming upon this coast when it arrived at *Krokala*. It is thus reasonable to assume that the 1000 *stadia* are to be reckoned from Krokala, or its vicinity, most likely from *Alexander's Haven* which was evidently close to *Krokala*, and whence, it may be said, the real start was made after the 24 days' detention. Taking this as the correct point of departure, the *paraplus* was as follows:

	Stadia		Distance to places conjecturally identified. Stat. miles.
Alexander's Haven to Domæ; or Observatory Island to a point 4 m. W. by N. from Karāchi native town	60	.	6
Domæ to Saranga, a few miles N. of Hab mouth	300	.	32
Saranga to Sakala, a little E. of Bidok Lak .	220	.	24
Sakala to Morontobara, Sirondha Lake . .	300	.	27
Morontobara to Arabius Mouth, Liāri . .	120	.	10
Total	1000	.	99

The equivalent of 1000 stadia is 100 geog. miles or 115 statute miles. Measurement round a coast on a map will certainly yield a shorter distance than that actually run by the vessels whose course is being traced, and no doubt a few miles may safely be added to the 99 above given, so that the estimates of Nearchus were wonderfully near the truth.

The result of this review of the early part of the voyage is to confirm Colonel Holdich's opinion as to the *latitude* of the Arabius mouth in those days. He, however, thinks it probable that the river farther north then ran much to the east of its present course. If this was so, all the requirements of my theory of the march of Alexander to the Arabius are satisfied. It is to be hoped that the investigation of the ancient topography of Southern Balochistān will be continued. The position of *Morontobara* requires, I think, farther consideration. I should incline to place it more to the east than Colonel Holdich does, though I am bound to feel much diffidence in dissenting from his opinion on such a point. The very name *Sirondha* may, I quite admit, be called in evidence on his side, and it would be worth while to make inquiry as to any local traditions connected with it.

But it will be seen that Colonel Holdich's opinion that the estimates of runs between Cape Monze and Morontobara (as identified by him) are excessive can hardly now be maintained. He has himself brought to light evidence which proves that these estimates approach much nearer to accuracy than, under all the circumstances, we could have expected. From the shortness of the runs for the first week after leaving Alexander's Haven it is most probable that in this part of its course the fleet had to depend on its oars alone. Here the longest day's run was 300 *stadia*. The weather seems to have been fine and the sea calm, since nothing to the contrary is stated. It is in the account of the eighth day's run (from Pagala to Kabana) that we first find mention of wind. On this occasion the fleet was caught by a *sudden* squall from the sea (πνεῦμα ὑπολαμβάνει τὰς νέας μέγα ἐκ πόντου. The suddenness is indicated by ὑπολαμβανει) in which three vessels were lost, and now we have a run of 400 (according to some copies, 430) *stadia*, and the estimates henceforth become excessive indeed. It is evident that as long as the mere rowing lasted the runs were estimated with remarkable correctness, but when sailing began the reckoning went altogether astray. It is probable that sails were hoisted for the first time during the run from Pagala when the north-east monsoon would favour the west-south-west course; hence the long run. The squall most likely struck the fleet when most of this run had been made, for the anchoring at evening at Kabana was but for a short time, and probably to await the subsidence of the wind and collect the wrecked crews who had swum ashore. At midnight the fleet weighed again and ran (probably under sail) 200 *stadia* to Kokala. These runs were no doubt immensely over-estimated, as was also the next one (to the Tomerus), put at 500 *stadia*, as well that following (to Malana), stated to be 300 *stadia*. The final result is that the *paraplus* along the coast of the Oritœ, that is, from the mouth of the Arabius (Purālī) to Malana (Cape Malan), is stated to be 1600 *stadia* in length, whereas measurement on a chart between these points shows the true distance to be only 850 *stadia!* Colonel Holdich seems to me to have fallen into a mistake in regard to the weather encountered by the fleet. With the exception of the squall above mentioned, which, it is clear, lasted but a short time, though long enough to wreck some of the crank craft of which the fleet was composed, the weather throughout the whole voyage from Alexander's Haven appears to have been excellent. Within a few hours after the squall the fleet was running before a fair and fresh breeze (ἔπλωον ἀκραεῖ) for the Tomerus, and after Masarna we find runs of 700, 800, and even 1000 *stadia* recorded—exaggerations, no doubt, but showing that in respect of weather all was going as well as could be wished. The hardships of the voyage were certainly extreme, but they arose from exposure, scanty provisions, bad water, hard toil, and long watches. All this would very likely have its effect on Nearchus' power of reckoning, but probably what chiefly vitiated his estimates was his over-rating the *sailing* capabilities of the tubs built on the Indus.

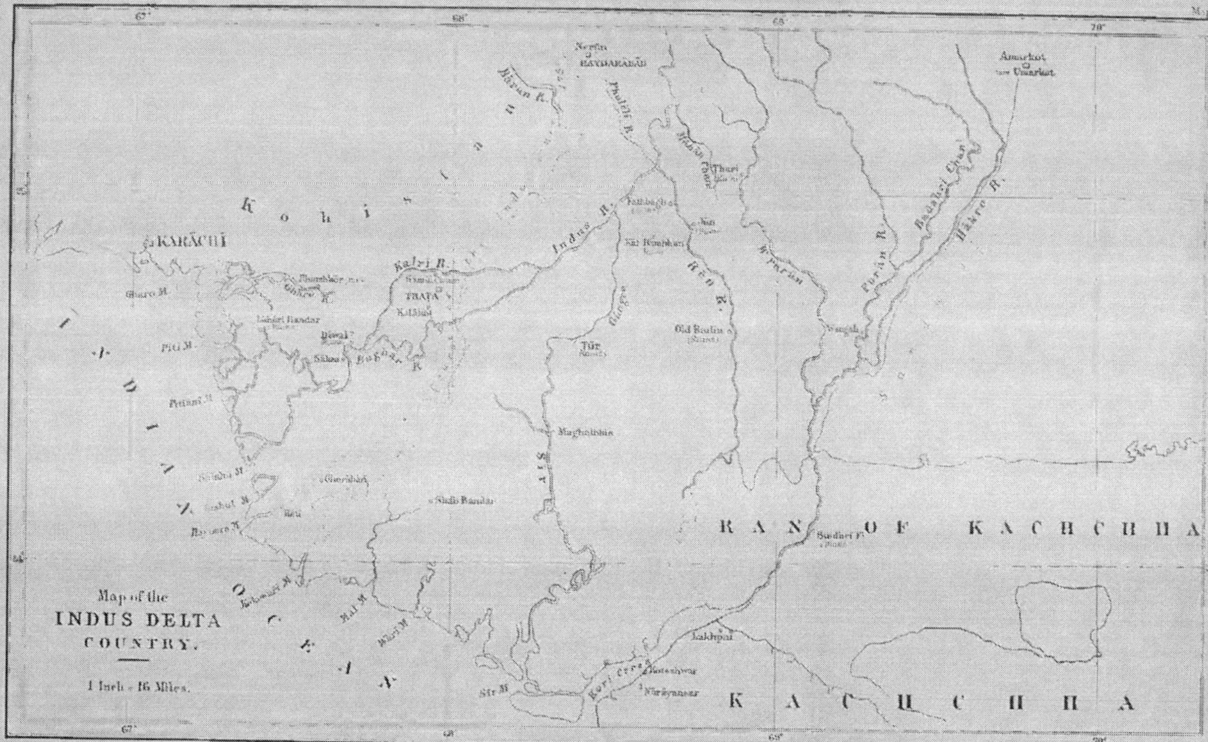
Map of the
INDUS DELTA
COUNTRY.
1 Inch = 16 Miles.
KARĀCHĪ
Kohistan
INDIAN OCEAN
Indus R.
Kalri R.
Baghar R.
TRATA
Ghāro R.
Lāhāri Bandar
Dewal
Ren R.
Old Badin
Tūr
Maghobhin
Sir
Sir M.
Kori Creek
Lakhpat
Nārāyansar
Sindhri F.
Vangah
Purān R.
Hākro R.
Amarkot
Nerūn
HAYDARĀBĀD
Phuleli R.
Bāran R.
Thari
Kāt Bambhan
Gūni R.
RAN OF KACHCHHA
KACHCHHA
67°
68°
69°
70°

Map II

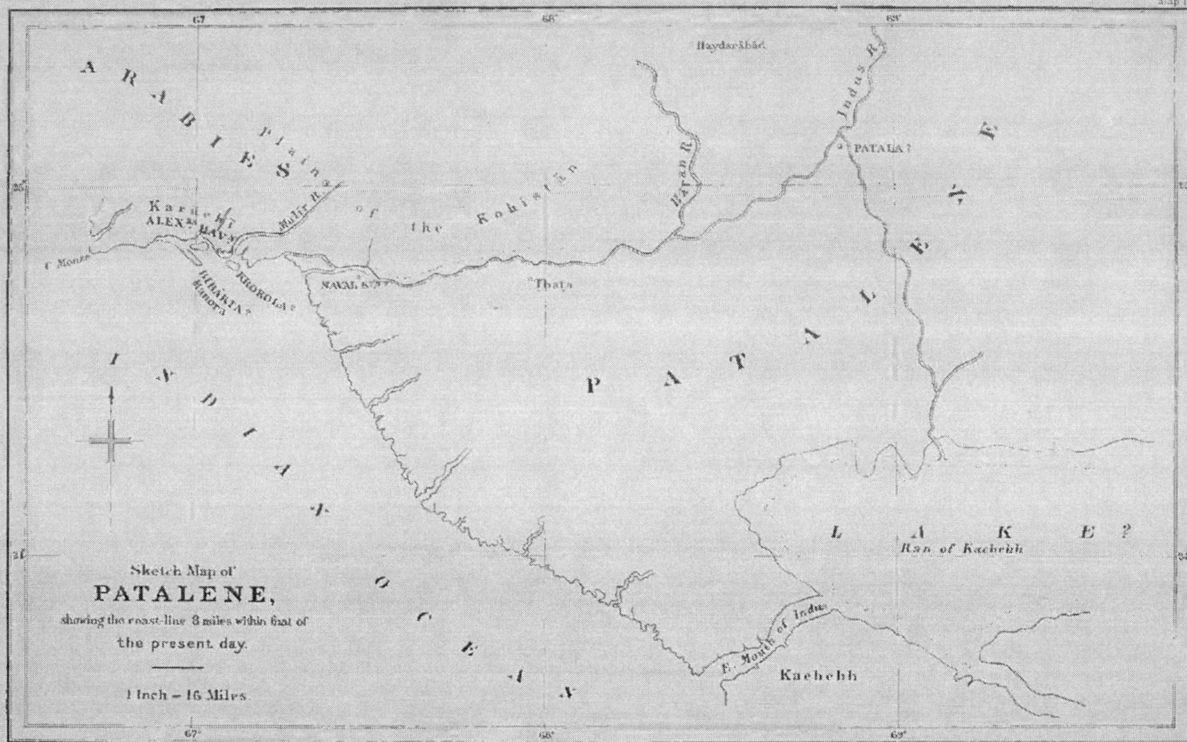

Sketch Map of
PATALENE,
showing the coast-line 8 miles within that of
the present day.
1 Inch = 16 Miles
ARABIES
Plains of the Kohistan
Karachi
ALEXRS HAVN
C. Monze
Malir R.
KROROLA ?
BIBAKTA ?
Manora
NAVAL ST.
Thata
Haydarabad
Indus R.
Baran R.
PATALA ?
PATALENE
INDIAN OCEAN
LAKE ?
Ran of Kachchh
E. Mouth of Indus
Kachchh
67°
68°
69°
25°
24°

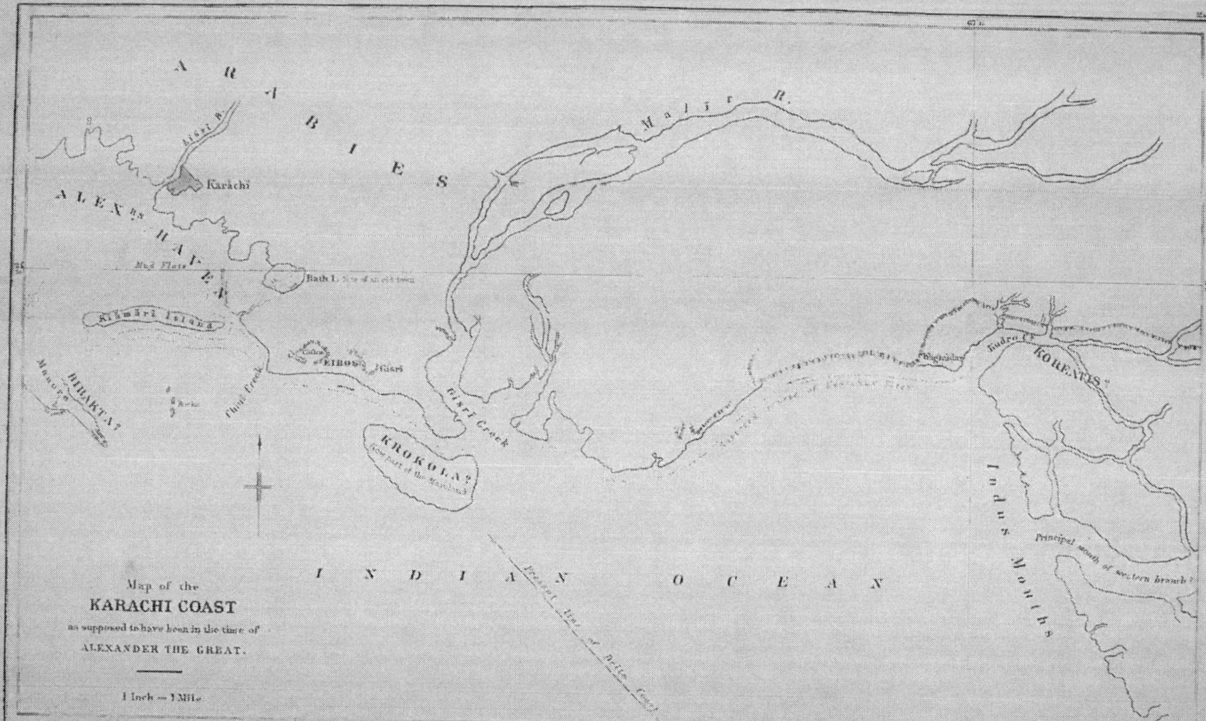

Map of the
KARACHI COAST
as supposed to have been in the time of
ALEXANDER THE GREAT.